"This cookbook dedicated to all my wonderful staff and the loyal customers over the past 25 years, who have supported me and have helped in making Hansa's Restaurant one of the iconic restaurants of Leeds and Yorkshire."

Hansa

Pictured from above, clockwise: The eating area upstairs in Hansa's Restaurant. Looking through the bar area downstairs. Hansa standing at the bar. A display of the popular salad buffet. Hansa demonstrating her cooking skills in one of her cookery demonstrations.

Hello & Namaste!

Welcome to Hansa's second cookbook!

Hansa's restaurant was established in 1986 and I am very proud to say that it is probably the only restaurant in Leeds still in the same hands after all these years.

The success in realising my dream is mainly down to my loyal and supportive customers who have helped make Hansa's a well recognised landmark of the Leeds restaurant scene.

With your continued support and encouragement I was able to publish Hansa's Indian Vegetarian Cookbook – popular recipes from Hansa's Gujarati Restaurant some eight years ago. Gaining confidence from your response and three reprints later, I am now embarking upon my writing and publishing a second book, with the hopes of similar support from all of you, my trusted readers. Not bad for a non-writer.

Encouraged by constant requests from my customers, I have now launched Hansa's Heritage Tours of India, organising escorted tours to India, especially my home state of Gujarat, to give you the opportunity to experience the lifestyle, culture and cuisine at first hand. I'm truly excited about these latest ventures and ask once again for your support.

Over the years I have had many accolades bestowed upon my style of cooking by media critics. The highlight being voted, 'Curry Chef of the Year in 2008', for the third time and being recognised for, 'Significant Contribution to the Leeds Restaurant Industry', by the Leeds Restaurants Association.

As time goes by I see my once youthful and enthusiastic student diners become parents in their own right and it is really pleasing to see them now continuing to visit our restaurant with their own children. A whole new generation of children are hopefully going to grow up without having any hang-ups about not enjoying a vegetarian meal.

Vegetarianism has now become a well accepted part of the British diet. What Hindus have been practicing from time immemorial is now being recognised and accepted as virtues of good and healthy living, without having to sacrifice on flavour.

The recipes that I have included in this cookbook are some of my all-time favourites, but have been slightly modified to suit most palates, whilst still maintaining the distinct Gujarati taste. I sincerely hope that you'll like what you'll be cooking and eating and there's no better compliment then seeing you using my recipes again and again.

Hansa

Salad bar photograph © Sue Hiscoe, all others © Rob Booker

1988

Best Indian Vegetarian Restaurant in UK

Good Curry Guide

2001/02

Leeds City Restaurant of the Year

Yorkshire Life

2002

Curry Restaurant of the Year

Leeds Guide Curry Chef Competition

2003

Asian Business Woman of the Year

Asian Business Development Network

2004

Curry Chef of the Year

Leeds Guide Curry Chef Competition

2007

Curry Chef of the Year

Leeds Guide Curry Chef Competition

2008

Outstanding Contribution to the Leeds Restaurant Industry

Leeds Restaurant Association

2009

Best Vegetarian Restaurant in UK

BBC Olive magazine

2010

The only Indian restaurant in Leeds recommended in

Good Food Guide 2010/11

❧ Foreword

I recently looked at the shortlist for an "Indian Restaurant of the Year" award and noted that not one of the establishments selected had its origins in India. All were excellent restaurants and were well-known for the quality of their food; all deserved to be there but the food they serve is not, in fact, from India. There is no doubt that Hansa's food is Indian and, more specifically, Gujarati. Everything my wife and I ate when we visited Gujarat on holiday seemed familiar. The recipes were not identical to Hansa's but, as we discovered, food changes every forty or fifty miles in India. Ingredients are grown, cooked and eaten in a small area. Those who have enjoyed a Thali at Hansa's Restaurant really will know what to expect in a restaurant or café in Ahmadabad. Some locals were surprised that we were as familiar with Gujarati cuisine and we were glad to tell them that we had been trained by the best.

I first ate at Hansa's in 1988 and fell in love with the food and the family-friendly atmosphere, rapidly becoming a regular diner. Our families soon became good friends. My son and her sons were young then and we have been pleased to watch them become adults. The restaurant has also changed in this time; new dishes have appeared on the menu and the fabric has been changed over the years. Some things are constant, though: the welcome to customers new and old is still warm, the food is freshly prepared, true to its Gujarati roots and as good as ever, and festivals, Christian as well as Hindu, are marked with special menus. The restaurant, like many of its original customers, has many of its original qualities and has aged well.

British people of Indian origin are generally less reluctant to speak of the good works of family and friends than are the wider population. As we have been invited to more and more events involving members of the Leeds Hindu community, I have learnt about the high regard in which Hansa, Kish and their family are held. People openly talk about the way in which Hansa's became a place at which people new to this country could find a welcome and eat food that reminded them of home. The restaurant, together with the Temple became a focal point for a growing community. Hansa's has provided employment for many, initially mainly Asian women, who, in the early years found it difficult to work outside the home. Generations of Leeds students from all over the world have been glad to work there too, and they and many customers have been encouraged to feel part of a generous and welcoming community. Hansa, who came to Leeds as a stranger in 1971, has become part of the established community and has helped others to do so too.

I was involved in the production of Hansa's first book and was delighted to see the finished product emerge from what started as a pile of pieces of paper. It was justly well-received and sold in quantities that surprised many. Some of the recipes are now regular features in the homes of our family and friends. I am delighted that Hansa has found time to produce a second selection of recipes. I have eaten most of them and am sure that they will prove to be as popular as their predecessors.

Alan Brown

Hansa's More Than Just A Restaurant! It's My Life!

First published in Great Britain in 2010 by Hansa's Publications.

PO Box 204

Leeds LS17 8WJ

England

Author: Hansa Dabhi

Publisher: Kishor Dabhi

Assistant Editors: Alan and Linda Brown

Art Director: Amanda Chauhan

Photography: Sue Hiscoe

Cover portrait photography: Rob Booker

Printed by: imageData Group, Grange Park Lane, Willerby, East Yorkshire HU10 6EB

Hansa's Restaurant, 72/74 North Street Leeds LS2 7PN

www.hansasrestaurant.com

ISBN: 9780953832613

Contents

✿ Looking Back

People always say that to appreciate what you have achieved in your life you should take time out to reflect on your past, by looking back to where you were at the different stages of your life and seeing where you are now. Only then you could measure the true progress of your life. When I look back to where I was born in 1956, in a small town called Fort Portal, on the southern shores of Lake Albert in Uganda, I can just about remember the two room hutment, which was all the space my parents could afford. It was where I grew up with six other children as well as mother and father. I sometimes wonder how did we manage it? Where did we all sleep, as I can only remember two small beds made with strong ropes tied in a crisscross fashion, around a rectangular wooden frame, which became the bedsprings and a hand made mattress, filled with cotton wool, to sleep on? How did my mum cope with all of us? How did we survive with only one person earning just enough money to feed, clothe and educate all of us? A small store room that doubled-up as a kitchen and storage for everything we possessed and a tiny bathroom and toilets outside the hutment was all the living space I was brought up in.

I am told that we were the lucky ones, as there were other Indian families who were worse off than us.

So how come we were so far from India, in a country we did not belong to, totally surrounded by native African people, whose language we could not speak and whose culture we did not understand? Well my father had joined the British Army as a young man, way back in 1940 and was posted to East Africa. Once he settled there he came back to India to collect my mother, my eldest brother and my eldest sister, to make a life in East Africa. Most other Indian soldiers and Indian migrants in those days settled in Kenya and would not dream of going beyond, but for some reason, my father decided to travel deeper into the African jungle to Kampala and then to Fort Portal, on the shores of Lake Victoria. Very few people survived this malaria ridden country, and I still cringe at the thought of what my parents and their two children would have been through in those days.

Above left: The opening of Hansa's Restaurant in May 1986 by Kapil Dev, captain of India's cricket team.

We lived here for nine years and my mother gave birth to three more daughters and two sons, me being the youngest of the daughters. Unfortunately, my youngest brother did not survive past his fifth birthday, so we were left with four sisters and two brothers in all.

We stayed in Fort Portal until 1964. My father had already left the army by then and was working as a carpenter. My elder brother Bhagwanji, left for Kampala looking for work and making a life for himself. My eldest sister Laliben, got married to my brother-in-law Naginbhai and moved to Kampala with him. After a year my father too decided to move to Kampala with all of us in tow, seeking better work opportunities. This was probably the worst move ever, as we were forced into abject poverty in the big city. Work for father was quite difficult to find, so mum ended up doing domestic work for other well-to-do families. One room was all we could afford, so that became the living room, the kitchen and the bedroom for all six of us.

After about four years in Kampala, we moved once again to a smaller town called Kakira, on the shores of Lake Victoria, quite close to a town called Jinja, famous for being at the source of River Nile, which Stanley and Dr.Livingstone had set off to discover, way back in the 19th Century.

Three years passed here in Kakira, which was a township run by the very rich sugarcane plantation owners called the Madhvanis. The Madhvanis owned a lot of the industries in Kakira and indeed most of Uganda, and employed lots of indentured Indian workers. They looked after their workers very well,

Left: Hansa receiving the Outstanding Contribution To The Leeds
Restaurant Industry Award 2008 by the Leeds Restaurant Association.
Above: The award winning team at Hansa's restaurant with
the Asian Business Woman of the Year Award 2003.

and that is how they could grow their business empire. They provided living accommodation, healthcare and education for all their workers, which were the only reasons why they all stayed in this mosquito ridden township. Many hundreds of people died of malaria every year, but it is amazing what people will put up with just for the sake of a bit of security, when work is so scarce.

Then came General Idi Amin Dada, a renegade soldier who overthrew the Ugandan government in an army coup and instantly set about dismantling and destroying the whole of the economy of Uganda. Within a year Uganda, which was world famous for its high quality coffee and being the most productive of the East African countries, now became a lawless nation, ravaged by tribal persecutions and economically bankruptcy, not able to feed its own people. We Indians became Idi Amin's prime target because most of the economic wealth was created and owned by us. He despised us because, like most migrants anywhere, we went along quietly with our daily living, in our own circles and would not mix with the native Ugandans. It was rumoured at the time that he wanted to marry one of the daughters of the Madhwanis and when he was turned down, he set about expelling all foreigners, using the army to use brutal force against us Indians, looting our property and raping our women. Thanks to the British Government of the day, that charter planes were sent to rescue the persecuted Indians before the date for evacuation set by the tyrant dictator.

We were luckier because my father had already immigrated to England in 1970, two years before Idi Amin came to prominence. As luck would have it, my brother Bhagwanji had negotiated a free plane ticket with a rich businessman for my father to come to England. In return my father had to bring the businessman's money out of the country legally and deposit it into his UK bank account.

My father settled in Leeds, where he knew some of our relations, who had come to the UK earlier. My brother Bhagwanji had again negotiated some more plane tickets for the rest of the family and so on 8th June 1971, the whole family was in the UK.

From left: Grand Master Chef Hemant Oberoi, Michelin & 5AA Rosette award-winning chef Jean Christophe Novelli, Barrington Douglas and Hansa pictured at the 2010 World Curry Festival.

What a shock to our system that was! From literally scraping a living, doing anything and any job to make a few shillings for our daily bread, to living in a four bed roomed terraced house, with a kitchen and outside toilets. There was one major problem for all of us, that of going for a proper wash only once a week, at the public baths. We were used to having a proper shower every morning and it felt very unclean. We used to boil water in the kettle for a quick wash every morning and go for a proper bath on Fridays after school, even in freezing winter conditions.

The ritual of lighting a coal fire every morning reminded me of how we had to light the 'Jeeko' back in Fort Portal. It was a simple version of a small cylindrical charcoal barbeque griddle, with a small window in the bottom chamber, which would be opened to let the air pass through the burning embers. We used to stuff the bottom chamber with newspapers and light it to create the flames to ignite the charcoal in the upper chamber. This Jeeko was our only source of cooking heat, on which all the food was cooked morning, noon and night. A permanent stone hearth was also a part of most households, where water for bathing and washing clothes, was heated in a large Aluminium drum or a smaller oil drum in our case, as we couldn't afford the Aluminium one.

One day father bought a new cooking utensil for mother, which was the latest way of cooking. It was called the Primus, which used paraffin in the bottom tank that needed to be pressurized by applying a few strokes to the piston pump, then a valve would be opened, very slowly, to release the pressurized paraffin up a tiny nozzle. A match would be applied and the whole thing would burst into a high powered jet flame. Instant heating! No more loading the charcoal and blowing into the bottom chamber of the Jeeko, to make the flames rise up to the charcoals, almost choking to death in the process! But we had many narrow escapes with the Primus stove as well, especially when putting the match to light the pressurized Paraffin initially. It would burst into flames instantly and we had to be very fast to move our hands and our clothing out of the way, in case it caught fire and maimed you for life. Many ladies were not that lucky. I know of cases in the Asian countries where mothers in laws would douse their supposedly unruly daughters in laws with paraffin and burn them and then point to the Primus stove as the cause of the accident.

Using the gas cooker hob back in Leeds was a completely new experience for us and an absolute godsend. We could cook tea at a minute's notice in relative safety. What a luxury!

I had just turned sixteen and soon joined reception courses at Park Lane College, with my sisters

© World Curry Festival

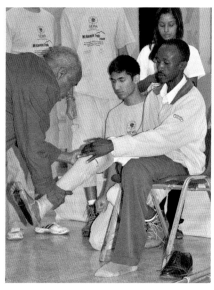

Far left: Hansa and party on top of Mt. Kenya on Sewa International's charity trek in 2009.
Left: A patient recieving artificial limb in Kenya, a project supported by Sewa International.

Pushpa and Damu and brother Kishor, to learn English for foreigners. This was quite easy for all of us because we had studied in an English medium school in Uganda, but it was the Yorkshire accent which took some time for us to master. The 'tele' helped a lot to learn to speak and listen to the spoken language and get to know the English culture, especially with shows like Coronation Street, which we watched religiously. I loved Tom Jones and Engelbert Humperdink! We used to finish all our house work well before their shows and would be really upset if we were to go visiting our relatives or anyone came visiting us at that particular time.

It was quite exciting for all of us to have more space for us to live in and to experience the first snowfall, which we had seen in the occasional movies on TV at our well-off neighbour's houses in Uganda. Getting used to people calling you "love" was a new experience for most of us Asians. It brought a little giggle for most of us since it is a word of endearment only reserved for someone very special, not for everyone you speak to, even complete strangers.

Soon my sisters and I were studying for the CSE exams and all left college after a year to take up jobs, me as a Lab Technician at Yorkshire Chemicals, my sister Pushpa as a Lab Technician at Burtons Clothing Factory and my sister Damu as a trainee nurse at the Leeds General Infirmary. My brother Kishor was still in the local secondary school. These new found jobs also gave us our first taste of freedom and economic independence, everything a teenager would relish, but also a lot of responsibilities too towards the rest of our family members.

My elder sisters would take up most of the important household chores so I was left to do smaller menial jobs in the house like cleaning up, ironing, preparing the vegetables, etc. It was only after I met and married Kishor, against my parents wishes, that I started to cook properly of my own accord. Kish's mother and sisters helped me a lot in developing my cookery skills and helped me be assimilated in my new home. As time went by, what I used to see mother do soon came back to me and I became very confident with myself.

Soon my two boys Manesh and Anand were born and I decided to give up my work at the Post Office Computer Centre and became a full time mother. Kishor became an engineering lecturer at

Bradford College and I took up part-time employment at the Harehills Housing Aid in Leeds, helping women through their housing and social problems and developed my understanding of the issues facing the male dominated Asian cultures. This was when I started thinking of starting my own business, which would be supported by women, who were dying to step out of the homes, even for a few hours, to experience life beyond the bounds of their four walls. Lots of women promised to support me if I was to start such a venture, where their inbuilt skills would be put to good use to make a living from. The idea of Hansa's Restaurant was born out of the needs of these women and my desire to put my culinary skills to the test. Over the next year Kish found a site on North Street, an old piano shop, and with money borrowed by remortgaging our house, we plunged into the venture with both feet, learning from our mistakes as we went along and supported by Kish's family and the women I had made friends with during this time.

Twenty four years on, I remember it like yesterday. The trials and tribulations of running a Vegetarian Restaurant in 1986 was quite a challenge. At first people had never heard the word Gujarati and some used to think that Hansa's was a German cooperative type outlet. Our family and friends kept encouraging us by being our first regular customers and helping us cope with the stresses of the day to day chores, like picking up our children from school and baby-sitting for us and stepping

in when our work load increased at the restaurant. This made us grow even closer to each other then before.

Fame and accolades soon followed and we got regular mentions in the media for being unique, which helped in keeping us motivated to strive for even better things. To date our restaurant has won awards for being 'The Curry Restaurant of the Year' several

In 2008 Hansa visited Saraswati Vidhyalaya's 'One teacher schools' supported by her during Hansa's Hertitage Tours to India.

Hansa's sons Manesh and Anand with their respective spouses Bina and Joanne.

years running, winning the 'Curry Chef of the Year' competition on three occasions, as well as commendations by the local and national newspaper food-critics on a regular basis. But the greatest accolade came last year when I and my restaurant was given the award for 'Outstanding Contribution to the Leeds Restaurant Industry', by the Leeds Restaurants Association, my peers. To me it was just reward for 'twenty three years of hard labour of love', where we have put Indian vegetarian cooking at the forefront of the dining public of the North as well as providing employment and support for hundreds of women over the years, who have moved onto better things, now that they have grown their own wings.

Hansa's Restaurant is now a place to visit for a special night-out for celebrating birthdays, anniversaries and other special occasions. People now request a vegetarian menu for their weddings, which would be completely unheard of back in the 80's and 90's. The Hansa's brand has also evolving into cookbooks, cookery lessons, snacks and now a tour company called Hansa's Heritage Tours, where we take small groups of our customers on escorted tours of India and my native Gujarat, to give them the experience of Indian culture, traditions and cuisine at first hand.

We have tried to pay back into society by supporting several charities over the years. At present Hansa's Restaurant is endeavouring to support one-teacher schools programme, run by Saraswati Vidhyalaya, in rural India and Nepal, run under the auspices of 'The 3Rs Education Trust' in the UK. We know that education opens the doors to opportunities and helps in eradicating poverty and ignorance forming a stepping stone to achieving self-sufficiency and self pride.

Looking back, I know that had it not been for the generosity of the British Government to rescue the Asians in the late 60's and the early 70's, we would probably not be alive today and the people of Yorkshire have particularly been kind and supportive to all of us as well. Despite the racism we experienced at the hands of the skin-heads in the earlier years, the majority of the people of Yorkshire stood by us when we needed them most. What a generous lot the British are! We Indians all regard

Britain as our true home and Yorkshire as 'Gods Own County', a real heaven on earth! Thank you all for making me what I am today.

The whole restaurant idea came about because we Hindus are vegetarian by and large, because Hinduism, like other religions, also says that 'thou shall not kill' and 'thou shall show respect for every living being on this earth'. Simply putting, Hindus believe in one Supreme God also, who has many manifestations. We have four goals in life, which we all aspire to live by - Dharma, Artha, Kaama and Moksha.

Hansa and Kishor.

Dharma meaning duty performed selflessly, ones duty to their family, friends, fellow workers, customers, the society, the environment and the planet. I have endeavoured to encompass all of these good karmas (actions) in my own life style and my vegetarian restaurant. We have achieved success in an ethical business which does not harm any living being, which provides work and support for my workforce as well as promoting good practical Hindu virtues amongst my clients too.

Artha (pronounced eartha) means economic wellbeing or accumulation of wealth by hard work and fair means. I am proud to say that achieving economic success has been a joint effort by everyone involved at Hansa's and doing it in an ethical manner is an even greater bonus. My biggest wealth is the accumulation of my customers, who are now a part of my family and also my closest friends. I feel truly wealthy!

Kaama means enjoyment of our senses and desires but with restraint and responsibility. Enjoying the taste of what I am cooking, enjoying creating new dishes for the future success of my business, enjoying the fruits of our labour, enjoying the love and affection I get from my work force, friends, family and my customers, but ensuring that I do not become boastful or selfish and loose my sense of duty to others.

Moksha (pronounced moxa) meaning achieving oneness with the almighty. We Hindus believe that you are born with certain privileges in the present life because you must have done certain deeds in your past life. Some people call it fate and I truly believe that I must have done some good deeds in my previous life, because of where I am today and what I have managed to achieve at various stages of my life. Saved from the jaws of death in Uganda, to living in this country, a true heaven on earth, to having a caring and supporting husband in Kish and my two loving sons, Manesh and Anand and their spouses Bina and Joanne, respectively, to enjoying the love and respect of my family members, to being surrounded by the most caring friends and customers one could ever wish for. No one could wish for any more! I will endeavour to keep on doing good Karmas in my present life, to ensure that my next incarnation will be equally as enjoyable as what I enjoy today. That will be true Nirvana for me! So help me God!

Hansa

Hansa's Heritage Tours

The idea of taking groups of people on tour of my beloved India was born out of the many requests by my customers, who wanted to visit India but felt a little apprehensive about going it alone. So now we organise guided tours to Gujarat and to Himachal Pradesh, visiting places off the beaten track to see and experience the lifestyle, the culture, the food and the people of India at first hand. A really exciting adventure for them and us as well. Most of our customers have come back with fantastic memories of the sights and sounds of India and can't stop talking about it. A few have gone back on their own, having overcome their fears and anxieties. Mission accomplished!

Sights and sounds of Gujarat & Himachal captured by fellow tourist.

Why Hindus don't eat meat

History

Vegetarianism has always been widespread in India is clear from the earliest Vedic texts. This was observed by the ancient traveler Megasthenes and also by Fa-Hsien, a Chinese Buddhist monk who, in the fifth century, travelled to India in order to obtain authentic copies of the scriptures.

The book FOOD FOR THE SPIRIT, VEGETARIANISM AND THE WORLD RELIGIONS, observes that, "Despite popular knowledge of meat-eating's adverse effects, the non-vegetarian diet became increasingly widespread among the Hindus after the two major invasions by foreign powers, first the Muslims and later the British. With them came the desire to be `civilized`, to eat as the Saheeb did. Those actually trained in Vedic knowledge, however, never adopted a meat-oriented diet, and many Hindus still observe vegetarian principles as a matter of their religious duty.

> *In the past fifty years, millions of meat-eaters - Hindus and non-Hindus - have made the personal decision to stop eating the flesh of other creatures.*

There are six major motivations for such a decision:

1. The Dharmic Law Reason
Ahinsa, the law of non-injury, is the Hindu's first duty in fulfilling religious obligations to God and God's creation as defined by Vedic scripture.

2. The Karmic Consequences Reason
All of our actions, including our choice of food, have Karmic consequences, ie reactions.

By involving oneself in the cycle of inflicting injury, pain and death, even indirectly by eating other creatures, one must in the future experience in equal measure the suffering caused.

3. The Spiritual Reason
Food is the source of the body's chemistry, and what we ingest affects our consciousness, emotions and experiential patterns. If one wants to live in peace and happiness and love for all creatures, then they cannot eat meat, fish, shellfish, fowl or eggs. By ingesting the grosser chemistries of animal foods, one introduces into the body and mind anger, jealousy, anxiety, suspicion and a terrible fear of death, all of which are locked into the flesh of the butchered creatures.

4. The Health Reason

Medical studies prove that a vegetarian diet is easier to digest, provides a wider ranger of nutrients and imposes fewer burdens and impurities on the body.

5. The Ecological Reason

Planet Earth is suffering. In large measure, the escalating loss of species, destruction of ancient rainforests to create pasture lands for live stock, loss of topsoil and the consequent increase of water impurities and air pollution have all been traced to the single fact of meat in the human diet.

6. Carbon Footprint Reason

Research has shown that the energy used in the rearing of the livestock and processing of the meat is equivalent to fourteen times that used in producing the same quantity of vegetables and grains. This can only get worst when the population of poorer nations start mimicking the lifestyle of the highly developed nations.

Why Hindus don't eat meat 19

ꙮ Ayurveda

"Let food be your medicine and let medicine be your food"

Now more than ever health conscious people are recognising the role good nutrition can play in our healing and our health. Ayurveda offers an insight into what foods will suit and balance each individual, how to prepare and cook food properly, how to avoid food combinations that can create toxins in the body, which eating habits to cultivate and avoid in order to gain the most nourishment from the food you eat.

Modern medicine increasingly encourages people to look at their lifestyles and the impact it has on their health and risk of illness. Anyone visiting India will come across Ayurveda and will realise that this ancient system also looks at lifestyle and diet. In my first book I gave a list of the healing properties of many of the ingredients which I use in my cooking and now I am including a very brief and simplified introduction to the Ayurvedic System of medicine, as I understand it. I hope that it will help the reader to gain a better understanding of this ancient philosophy as well. If you would like to know more, there are many excellent books on the subject as well as information on the internet sites devoted to the subject such as www.holisticonline.com or www.ayuspa.co.uk. It is most important that you consult an Ayurvedic physician, especially if you suffer from certain allergies or conditions.

Understanding Ayurveda

Introduction   Ayurveda is India's traditional, holistic system of medicine that has been practiced for more than 5,000 years. Ayurveda is a Sanskrit word that literally translated means "science of prolonging life". It was the system of health care conceived and developed by the seers (rishis) and nature scientists through centuries of observations, experimentations, discussions and meditations. For several thousand years their teachings were passed down orally from teacher to student. In about the fifth to sixth century BC, elaborately detailed texts were written by rishis Charaka, Sushruta, and Vagbhata in Sanskrit, the ancient language of India, giving detailed descriptions of the various practices. Rishi Charaka listed 500 hundred remedies and rishi Sushruta over 700 vegetable medicines. Ayurveda flourished and was, and still is, used by the rich and the poor alike in India and Southeast Asia.

Concept of Tri-Dosha

In Ayurvedic philosophy, the five elements Air, Ether, Water, Fire and Earth combine in pairs to form three dynamic forces or interactions called Doshas. They are:

Doshas	Related Elements
VATA	Consisting of the elements Air and Ether
PITTA	Consisting of the elements Fire and Water
KAPHA	Consisting of the elements Water and Earth

Dosha means "that which changes". Ones Dosha is determined at the time of conception or the inherited genetic coding. The Doshas are constantly moving in dynamic balance, one with the others. In Ayurveda, every living thing in nature is characterised by its Dosha.

It places particular emphasis on the individual's constitution *(prakruti)* which is determined by the unique combination of Doshas. *Prakruti* determines an individual's susceptibility to different diseases and has an influence on their course and development. *Vikruti* concentrates on determining the imbalance of your Doshas. The Ayurvedic practitioner will usually try to determine the amount of this imbalance, which in turn will help to determine the state of your wellbeing, then prescribe you the treatment consisting of herbal medicines, recommend lifestyle changes needed and simple Yoga exercises to do bring back the balance of your Doshas. It is not a quick fix dose of fast acting medication which we are used to here in the West. A complete lifestyle change is recommended for the body and mind to work together as a whole to heal you.

Vata is a force conceptually made up of elements ether and air

The proportions of ether and air determine how active Vata is. The amount of ether (space) affects the ability of the air to gain momentum. If unrestricted, as in the ocean, air can gain momentum and become an uncontrollable force such as a hurricane.

Vata means "wind, to move, flow, direct the processes of, or command." Vata enables the other two Doshas to be expressive. The actions of Vata are drying, cooling, light, agitating and moving.

Vata governs breathing, blinking of the eyelids, movements in the muscles and tissues, pulsations in the heart, all expansion and contraction, the movements of cytoplasm and the cell membranes and the movement of the impulses in nerve cells. Vata also governs such feelings and emotions as freshness, nervousness, fear, anxiety, pain, tremors and spasms. The primary seat or location of the Vata in the body is the colon. It also resides in the hips, thighs, ears, bones, large intestine, pelvic cavity and skin. It is related to the touch sensation. If the body develops an excess of Vata, it will accumulate in these areas.

Pitta is a force created by the dynamic interplay of water and fire

These forces represent transformation. They cannot change into each other but they modulate or control each other and are vitally required for the life processes to occur, for example, too much fire and too little water will result in the boiling away of the water. Too much water will result in the fire being put out.

Pitta governs digestion, absorption, assimilation, nutrition, metabolism, body temperature, skin coloration, the lustre of the eyes, intelligence and understanding. Psychologically, Pitta arouses anger, hate, and jealousy. The small intestine, stomach, sweat glands, blood, fat, eyes and skin are the seats of Pitta.

Kapha is the conceptual equilibrium of water and earth

Kapha is structure and lubrication. One can visualise the Kapha force as the stirring force to keep the water and earth from separating. For example, if we take a pot, half fill it with water and then add sand to it, the sand will gradually sink to the bottom of the pot. It separates from the water. The only way to keep the sand in equilibrium with the water is by stirring the mixture continuously. The Kapha force can be visualised as this stirring force in our body. Kapha cements the elements in the body, providing the material for physical structure. This dosha maintains body resistance. Water is the main constituent of Kapha and this bodily water is responsible for the biological strength and natural tissue resistance in the body. Kapha lubricates the joints, provides moisture to the skin, helps to heal wounds, fills the spaces in the body, gives biological strength, vigour and stability, supports memory retention, gives energy to the heart and lungs and maintains immunity. Kapha is present in the chest, throat, head, sinuses, nose, mouth, stomach, joints and in the liquid secretions of the body such as mucus. Psychologically, Kapha is responsible for the emotions of attachment, greed and long-standing envy. It is also expressed in tendencies toward calmness, forgiveness and love. The chest is the seat of Kapha.

Determine your Prakruti - constitution

Here is your chance to determine your Prakruti or constitution and, therefore, your active Doshas. Use the chart below and tick or list the various characteristics which you can recognise in yourself - be honest! Then add the ticks in each column. This will determine which Dosha is dominant and which is the second most influential Dosha in your Prakruti. Everyone has characteristics of all three Doshas but it is the ratio or dominance that determines your Prakruti. If you have scored 6 Kapha, 4 Vatas and 2 Pittas your constitution is Kapha/Vata, with Kapha as your dominant Dosha. You can now follow the Kapha dietary habits outlined below but also consider the Vata elements as well.

(Please note that this is only a small part of the full list of characteristics the Ayurvedic practitioner would use during consultation to determine your Prakruti.)

Characteristics	VATA (colon)	PITTA (stomach)	KAPHA (chest)
Mind Function	Quick mind, often restless	Sharp intellect, can get aggressive	Usually calm, steady disposition
Memory	Short term is best	Good general memory	Good long term memory
Thoughts	Constantly changing	Fairly steady	Steady
Eating habits	Eats quickly	Medium speed	Eats slowly
Personal tendencies	Worrier, anxious type, fearful or insecure	Enjoys challenges but easily frustrated	Calm, not easily stressed avoids arguments
Decision making	Difficulty in making decisions	Makes firm, good decisions	Slow in making decisions
Concentration levels	Short term concentration is best	Better than average concentration	Can focus for long periods
Personal make-up	Hyperactive - juggling a lot of tasks	Moderate physical activity	Serentary lifestyle - can be lazy
Body structure	Finds it hard to gain weight	Medium weight, evenly distributed	Tendency to gain weight
Body temperature	Usually suffers from cold hands and feet	Warm or hot skin temperature	Cool body temperature
Sleeping habits	Interrupted/light sleeper	Sound medium length sleeper	Needs sound, heavy, long sleep

VATA - *Balancing Diet*

Vata being the air Dosha tends to be flighty in their habits. When out of balance they often eat irregularly, quickly or not at all. The balancing diet should contain foods that are nutritious rather than just 'fast or convenient' to bring back the enjoyment in their eating and Doshic balance.

Vata Dietary Recommendations: People with Vata dominant Dosha have an unpredictable appetite and an inherent dislike for routine.

Key qualities of a good Vata diet are: warm, heavy, moistening, nourishing, soothing, satisfying and grounding. Warm foods are best.

Eat warm and thoroughly cooked meals and easily digestible foods such as stews and simple one-pot meals, eating raw vegetables and unripe fruits sparingly.

Use warming spices such as ginger, garlic, cumin, turmeric, black pepper, asafoetida (hing) and a little salt to help prime digestion.

Vata people have low tolerate to vegetables such as potatoes, tomatoes, peppers, eggplant and are often lactose tolerant as well.

Vata is aggravated by aging, in the autumn season, afternoon time, during travel, loud music, cold and windy conditions. Care should be taken during these times and conditions.

Qualities of food that bring balance back to you are: sweet, heavy, sour, salty, oily and warm foods. Use proportionately more of these food items.

Qualities of food that unbalance you are: pungent, bitter, astringent, light, dry and cold foods. Take less of these food items.

Eat three or four small meals a day at three to four hour intervals, starting with a good breakfast and taking hot milk at night to help with sound sleep.

Watch out for signs of poor digestion such as constipation, gas, bloating, restlessness or heaviness in the head or limbs. If these symptoms arise eat very lightly until the digestion is back to normal.

PITTA - *Balancing Diet*

Pitta is associated with heat and Pitta people often believe that their digestive fire can consume virtually anything, resulting in overestimating what their digestive system can handle, leading to ulcers and other gastro-intestinal problems.

Pitta Dietary Recommendations: People with a dominant Pitta Dosha usually have a strong appetite that needs to be satisfied regularly. If left unsatisfied it could lead to intense hunger or irritation or anger.

Key qualities of a good Pitta diet are: cool, slightly dry (not soggy or oily) and a little heavy diet with minimum salt.

Eat the main meal or at least a good sized meal at midday, avoiding late night eating.

Fresh fruit or vegetables are the best evening snacks if needed to combat hunger pangs.

Avoid eating excessively greasy or rich and hot spicy food. Red meat, eggs, alcohol, caffeine and sugar must also be avoided.

Qualities of food that bring balance to you are: sweet, astringent, bitter, cool, heavy and dry foods. Take proportionately more of these food items.

Pitta increases during summer, midday and midnight, during intense heat or sunlight. They should be mindful at these times.

Eat three meals a day at regular times leaving four hours gap between meals, starting with a light breakfast and an early lunch.

KAPHA - *Balancing Diet*

Kapha is a cold and moist Dosha related to the elements of Earth and Water. Kapha balancing foods should be light and warm countering the tendency towards heaviness and inertia. Spicy foods are beneficial as they tend to speed up the often sluggish digestion.

Kapha Dietary Recommendations are: People with Kapha dominance should eat small portions of high quality of food to balance your Dosha, taking low salt, low fat, high fibre and lightly cooked foods.

Key qualities of Kapha people are that they are the only ones who could happily skip breakfast. Eating between 10am and 6pm is best.

Avoid sleeping after meals as this adds heaviness in the body. Take a gentle walk instead.

Do a liquid fast once a week and be mindful of not using food for emotional support as this would cause weight gain, especially consuming chocolate and late night ice cream.

Kapha is increased in early morning, late evenings and in spring. Be most careful with your diet at these times, avoiding heavy breakfast or late night kitchen raids.

Qualities of food that bring balance to you are: pungent, light, dry, astringent, bitter and hot food items. Take proportionately more of these food items.

Qualities of food that unbalances you are: sweet, heavy, sour, oily, salty and cold food items. Take less of these food items and less frequently.

Best to eat twice a day at midday and early evenings, with at least 5–6 hours gap in between meals, only taking juice or herbal tea for breakfast and avoid coffee in the morning.

These guidelines are for general knowledge only, what I myself understand about Ayurveda and its practices. I hope that these will create enough interest in the reader to find out more about what Ayurveda has to offer them and help them to regain control over their bodily functions on a day to day basis.

Mari-Masala - Spices

Indian cooking cannot exist without spices. The Ayurvedic approach dictates that spices should be used sparingly to enhance the taste of the vegetables and the pulses as well as promote the physical wellbeing of the individual. There is a tendency in the West of demanding the use of extra spices in order to make the curry very potent, with the obvious effects on the gastric and the digestive systems. Stomach ulcers and heartburn are the two most common immediate effects on the body any such over-indulgences. Chillies used in small quantities are known to alleviate arthritic pains but can also cause stomach ulcers and gastric problems when taken in larger quantities. I have included many such medicinal tips throughout the book to bring this point home.

The list of spices is endless but I have restricted myself to the use of spices that are easily available in the local Asian grocery shops and supermarkets. Most of the spices nowadays are cleaned and packaged to a very high standard and it always pays to try out the spices blended by different manufacturers until you find the one that gives you the best results.

The content of my masala tin (spice-tin) are as follows:
Turmeric (hardar) powder, red chilli powder (lal marcha-ni bhukhi), cumin and coriander mixture (dhanna-jeeru), garam masala, salt (nimakh), mustard seeds (rai), cumin seeds (jeeru), carom seeds (ajmo), fenugreek seeds (methi), cloves (laving), cinnamon (taj), cardamon (elchi) and dried red chillies (sukha lal marcha).

Fresh green spices include ginger, garlic and green chillies. They are best prepared as the cooking begins although they can also be prepared and frozen in an ice-tray and used a cube at a time as required.

The herbs most commonly used in my cooking are coriander, fenugreek and dill.

Chilli powder *(marcha-ni-bhukhi):* This is available in two strengths, hot and extra hot, so use it according to your personal preference. The quantities I have used would make a mild curry but please do experiment until you achieve the taste that you like.

Cumin seeds *(jeeru):* These are brownish seeds with a likeness to caraway seeds. Cumin seeds are used in vegetable and rice dishes to give them a rich aromatic flavour. Dry roasted cumin seeds, coarsely ground or crushed, give raitas and lassis a very special taste.

Turmeric *(hardar):* This is a yellow powder used mainly to give the curries the distinctive rich yellow colour. It must be used in very small quantities to avoid overpowering the curry with its strong bitter after taste. Turmeric, especially when mixed with oil, will easily stain the work surfaces and clothing so avoid spilling it or handling it with bare hands.

© Rob Booker

Cumin and coriander powder *(dhanna-jeeru):* This is available ready mixed or they can be bought separately. I prefer to mix my own, in equal quantities, as I find that the ready mixed ones tend not to be equally balanced.

Garam masala: Garam masala, meaning hot mixture, is a mixture of at least ten different spices mixed in varying quantities. Every Gujarati household has its own recipe for making garam masala to suit their own taste. Mine will remain a closely-guarded secret but my garam masala will be available on request. You can also purchase it ready mixed from most Asian grocery shops.

The garam masala can be used at the cooking stage or as a garnish. It tends to change the colour of the curry to a darker shade so use it sparingly. Daals and pulses benefit the most from garam masala as they tend to be rather bland in taste.

Mustard seeds *(rai):* These tiny purplish brown seeds have a very powerful bitter taste and a small quantity of the seeds is used to flavour the curry by first sizzling them in some hot oil until they pop and then mixing the rest of the

ingredients in it. This process is known as 'waghaar'.

Mustard seeds are mainly used with vegetable curries and certain dry daal curries.

Carom seeds *(ajmo):* These tiny brown seeds are a member of the cumin family. Flavoursome carom seeds are sizzled in hot oil before adding certain beans to it, such as vaal and black eyed beans, to ease the digestion of these beans.

Fenugreek seeds *(methi):* These are tiny mustard coloured seeds with a very bitter taste. They can be used whole or crushed. The whole seeds must be sizzled in hot oil before adding the vegetables or daals to it or can be used crushed for pickles.

Cloves *(laving):* This pretty looking spice almost resembles a tiny flower but has a very strong aromatic flavour. I tend to use it whole to flavour some rice dishes, kadhi and daal sauces and the garam masala of course.

Cinnamon *(taj):* The bark of the cinnamon tree has a slightly sweet aromatic taste and is used like the cloves to flavour the rice dishes and the vegan desserts such as lapsi and sev. It is also one of the main ingredient of the chai masala (spicy tea mixture).

Cardamon *(elchi):* Cardamon comes in green, white or black pods. The seeds of the green and the white pods are used to enhance the flavour of rice dishes, some hot desserts and some pulses. The seeds of these pods are crushed or ground and used as a garnish for most of the Indian desserts.

The larger black cardamon is used as one of the ingredients of the garam masala.

Set Menu Suggestions

Many people are at a loss as to which dishes to make for a dinner party because they are unsure which of the food items would complement each other. Here I have suggested three set menus which would provide a good variety of tastes and textures. These would take away your anxieties and leave good memories for your guests as well.

There is also a list of 3 snacks below which are fairly easy to make for when you are feeling a little peckish.

Menu 1

Starter
Patudi - p48

Main Courses
Ringan Paletta - p70 and Channa - p79 curries
served with plain rice, daal and rotli

Dessert
Jeera Ananas - p147

Menu 2

Starters
Bateta Vada - p42

Main Courses
Bhaji Paneer - p65 and Urad - p84 curries
served with Coriander rice and baturas

Dessert
Kheer - p144

Menu 3

Starter
Paneer Tiki - p39

Main Courses
Ringan Bharta - p67 and Chevti Daal - p81
served with Jeera rice and puris

Dessert
Tropical Fruit Salad - p145 with
Vanilla ice-cream

Snacks Menu Suggestions

Pau Bhaji - p44

Mogo - p53

Methi-na-Dhebra - p110

Pictured clockwise from top left: Channa, Chevti Daal, Jeera Ananas and Mogo.

"Hansa you are one of the greatest Indian Vegetarian style chefs."

Jean-Christophe Novelli

Jean-Christophe Novelli is a Michelin and 5AA Rosette award winning French chef

"Hansa's is famous in Leeds for the right reasons.
If there's better veggie food, I've never tasted it."

Nick Miles

Emmerdale Farm's Jimmy King

"Well Hansa, it's your life and now it's mine. Quite simply the
best food I've had in Leeds!! I'm not a vegetarian,
but you could turn me into one. Love!"

Nicola Wheeler

Emmerdale Farm's Nicola King

"I came here in 1986 when I was working for Yorkshire Women
Theatre Co. I fell for your Patra and have been in love ever since.
It's still as good! Mmm..... lush! Love!"

Charlie Hardwick

Actress

Gujarati Starters

This section contains my very popular snacks which are served as starters and specialities in my restaurant. I have included some of my own creations like the Mushroom Special and the stuffed tomato special Hansa's Delight.

Each of the recipes is made for serving four diners and is served with chutney accompaniments which are listed in the chutneys and pickles section.

Index cards throughout © pictac/istockphoto®

Hansa's Delight

My own, creation using a spicy paneer filling in a tomato, one of the most popular starters at my restaurant. The filling can be substituted with a spicy mashed potato and sweet-corn mixture, if you are vegan or allergic to dairy products.

SERVES 4

PREPARATION TIME 15 MINS COOKING TIME 20 MINS

Filling:

4 medium beef tomatoes – *cut top and scoop out the seeds from the core*
4 spring onions – *finely chopped*
1 tsp garlic – *minced*
1 tsp green chilli – *minced*
125g paneer - *grated*
1 tsp salt

2 tsp jeera
2 tbsp oil - *for tempering*

Batter:

250g gram flour
140ml water
1 tsp salt
Oil for deep-frying

Method for the filling

1 Take a bowl and add the grated paneer, spring onions, garlic, salt, green chillies and mix well.

2 Heat the oil in a pan, add the Jeera and stir-fry till brown, then add the paneer mixture to this tempered oil and mix well again.

3 Stuff this filling in the cored tomatoes.

4 Make the batter by mixing all the ingredients together to form a smooth paste, not too runny.

5 Heat the oil for deep-frying.

6 Cover the tomatoes with the batter by dipping and slide it gently in the hot oil and fry it until golden brown.

7 Slice the tomato in half and serve it on a bed of salad with a tomato and mint chutney.

Smita's Khasta Kachori

This is a particularly sumptuous starter, worth the extra time and effort required to make it, but the result is a very beautifully presented offering, that can be the pride of any dinner table.

SERVES 4

PREPARATION TIME 30 MINS   COOKING TIME 30 MINS

Filling:	Dough:	Garnishing:
110g maag daal – *shelled*	110g plain flour	1 tbsp tamarind sauce *(see recipe)*
1 tsp red chilli powder	1/2 tsp salt	1 tbsp pepper chutney *(see recipe)*
1 tsp salt	2 tbsp oil	1 tbsp coriander and mint chutney *(see recipe)*
2 tsp coriander powder	100ml water	1 medium red onion – *finely chopped*
1/2 tsp garam masala		110g sev – *fine variety*
2 tsp fennel seeds		5 sprigs fresh coriander – *finely chopped*
1/2 medium lemon – *juice of*		

Method for the filling

1 Soak the Maag daal for 3 hours, washed and drained.

2 Coarsely grind the daal in a food processor.

3 Heat the oil in a pan, add the maag daal, all the spices mixing it well and let it cook for 10 mins, on a low heat, stirring frequently.

4 Remove from the heat and let it cool down.

5 Divide the filling into 6 equal portions.

Method for the dough

1 In a suitable bowl add the flour, salt, oil and mix well.

2 Gradually add water and make the dough, kneading it to form a smooth soft dough.

3 Divide the dough into 6 equal portions and knead it well.

Method for the Kachoris

1 Take one dough ball and roll it into an 8cm round.

2 Place one portion of the filling in the middle and bring the sides to enclose it, sealing it on the top by removing any excess dough. Repeat the process to make the other 5 balls.

3 Flatten the ball slightly by applying a little pressure, then roll out the stuffed dough slowly into a 12cm rounds to form a Kachori. Repeat the process to make all the Kachoris.

4 Deep fry the Kachoris, on a moderate heat, till slightly brown on both sides, patting it on the surface gently with a slotted spoon, to encourage it to balloon up.

5 To serve, place the Kachori on the serving plate, break open the top and garnish it with Sev, then lace it with the tamarind sauce, green and the red chutney, red onions and the coriander.

Spice Bomb

As it says, it'll blow your mouth with the tasty, spicy sensation that will warm you inside out. It's my own creation that is very popular with my adventurous, dare-devil customers who wanted something very spicy but tasty as well.

SERVES 4

PREPARATION TIME 10 MINS COOKING TIME 20 MINS

8 small potatoes – *boiled, peeled and cooled*
8 whole green chillies
Oil for deep frying

Batter:

110g gram flour
1/2 tsp salt
140ml water

Filling:

110g ganthiya – savoury gram flour nibble (available in shops)
2 tbsp red chilli powder
1 tsp sugar
2 sprigs fresh coriander – *finely chopped*
1/2 medium lemon – *juice of*
2 tbsp oil

Method for the filling

1 Soak the Ganthiya in water for 20 mins then drain off the water and mash it in the paste.

2 Add the rest of the ingredients and mix well. The filling is ready.

Method for the batter

1 Add the salt and the water to the gram flour and whisk it to a smooth paste, not too runny.

Method for making the Spice Bomb

1 Cut the boiled potatoes in half, lengthways and hollow out the potato with a spoon or something similar.

2 Fill both the potato halves with the spicy filling then place a whole green chilli length-ways with the stalk of the chilli sticking out and close the two halves.

3 Heat the oil for frying to a moderate heat and check it for the correct temperature by dropping a few drops of the batter in the oil. If the batter rises immediately to the surface, the oil is ready.

4 Hold the potato sandwich firmly and dip it in the batter until it is evenly covered all over.

5 Gently slide it into the hot oil at the shallow edge of the frying pan. and fry it till golden brown.

6 Serve it on a bed of lettuce with our tomato and mint chutney.

Paneer Tiki or Vegetable Tiki

Tikis are very popular and tasty cutlets which can have many different fillings. I have chosen Paneer filling. Tikis are made at special celebration parties, served with various chutneys and make a great starter when served with salad.

For Vegan or those allergic to dairy products, the Paneer filling could be substituted by a mixture of savoury peas, carrots and sweet-corn.

SERVES 4

PREPARATION TIME 30 MINS   COOKING TIME 30 MINS

Small potatoes - *boiled, skinned and mashed*

2 tbsp gram flour

2 tbsp corn flour

2 tsp green chillies - *minced*

2 tsp sugar

1½ tsp salt

2 sprigs coriander - *finely chopped*

Oil for deep frying

Ingredients for the filling:

100g paneer *(Indian cheese)* – *coarsely grated (can be replaced by 50g peas, 50g sweet-corn kernels (both coarsely ground) and 1 grated carrot)*

2 tsp sugar

1 tsp green chillies – *minced*

½ tsp garlic – *minced*

½ tsp salt

½ tbsp oil

1 tsp jeera

2 sprigs coriander – *finely chopped*

½ lemon - *juice off*

Method

1 Take the mashed potato and mix well with the gram flour, corn flour, salt, green chillies, sugar, coriander and lemon juice, then make 20 equal balls and set aside for later.

2 For the filling take the grated paneer (or vegetable mixture), sugar, green chillies, garlic, salt, coriander and lemon juice then mix well.

3 In a pan heat the oil and stir-fry the Jeera for 30 sec then add the above mixture to the pan and mix well, then take it off the heat to cool down and divide it into equal 10 portions.

4 Take 2 portions and flatten them into flat round discs between the palms of your hands.

5 Place one of the paneer balls in between the 2 potato discs and seal the edges with your finger tips then mould it into a ball shape, using a circular motion of your hands and flatten it slightly. This is now known as a Tiki. Make 9 Tikis with the remainder of the mashed potato balls.

6 Heat the oil to moderate heat and deep fry the Tikis till golden brown then remove it and place it on a paper towel to soak up the excess oil, before serving it with coriander and mint chutney.

The happy chefs at Hansa's

Bateta Vada

A most popular starter which takes minutes to make and serve. It is enjoyed by adults and children alike and can be made as spicy or as mild as you like. The textures can be varied by adding different ingredients to the mixture to your liking. The beauty about this starter is that you can have all the mixture for the filling and the batter made earlier and then deep-fry the vadas as and when required.

SERVES 4

PREPARATION TIME 20 MINS   COOKING TIME 20 MINS

Stuffing Mixture:

4 small potatoes – *boiled, peeled and mashed, then cooled*
1/2 tsp salt
1 tsp green chillies – *minced*
2 tbsp sugar
1/2 tsp cinnamon powder
2 sprigs coriander – *finely chopped*
1/2 lemon - *juice of*

50g peanuts – *crushed (optional)*
50g sweet-corn kernels – *coarsely chopped (optional)*
Oil – *for deep-frying*

Batter:

100g gram flour
1/2 tsp salt
100ml water

Method

1   Take a medium sized mixing bowl and add the mashed potato mix, peanuts (optional), green chillies, sugar, cinnamon powder, salt and coriander. Add lemon juice and mix well.

2   *(Optional)* - You may add the sweet-corn here, to give a different texture and taste

3   Make about 20 round balls from the mixture.

4   Take a small bowl and add the gram-flour, water and salt and make a smooth batter, not too thick.

5   Heat the oil in a deep-frying pan, to a moderate heat.

   Tip: *To test the correct temperature, drop a droplet of the batter into the oil. If it rises to the surface quickly, then the oil is ready for frying.*

6   Dip a few of the balls into the batter, then lift out one ball at a time and roll it in your fingers to let the excess batter drip off, then slowly slip the ball into the hot oil. Do the same with the other balls and fry a few Vadas at a time for 2-3 mins, turning them with a slotted spoon, until they are golden brown in colour. Remove the fried Vadas and place them on a plate covered with kitchen roll to soak up the excess oil. Serve hot with tomato and mint chutney.

Mushroom Special

This is an East - West creation that would appeal to anyone who likes spicy mushrooms served on a potato Rosti or other such base of your own liking. It looks very appetising when presented well.

SERVES 4

PREPARATION TIME 20 MINS COOKING TIME 30 MINS

Closed mushrooms – *sliced*
Small onion – *thinly sliced*
1 tbsp tomato puree
1 tsp salt
1 tsp red chilli powder
1/2 tsp garlic – *minced*
1/2 tsp garam masala
3 tbsp oil

Ingredients for the Rostis:

3 medium potatoes –
par-boiled and grated
1/2 tsp salt
Oil for shallow frying

Method for the mushrooms

1 Heat the oil in a frying pan and stir-fry the garlic first then add the sliced onions and fry till soft but not brown.

2 Add the tomato puree, salt and chilli powder, mix well and then add the mushrooms. Cook at a gentle heat for 10 mins, stirring frequently.

Method for the rostis

1 Add the salt to the grated potato and mix well, then take a small amount of the potato and form small round flat rostis for the mushroom.

2 Shallow fry these flat rostis, turning on both sides till golden brown then place on paper towel to soak up the excess oil.

3 To serve, place the cooked mushroom mixture on each rosti and serve with salad and apple chutney.

Tip: *You can buy ready made Rostis if you do not have time to spare.*

 # Pau Bhaji

This is a simple yet tasty snack, easily cooked with everyday ingredients found in most homes. It is a very commonly found as street food in most Indian cities. It is popular with adults and children alike.

SERVES 4

PREPARATION TIME 30 MINS COOKING TIME 15 MINS

1 small potato – *peeled, and diced*
100g cauliflower – *separate florets*
1/2 carrot – *diced*
1/2 dutch aubergine – *cut into small chunks*
100g garden peas
2 fresh tomatoes
1 tsp ginger – *minced*
1 tsp garlic – *minced*
1 tsp salt
1/2 tsp tumeric
1 tbsp tomato puree

1 tbsp whole cumin seed
100g butter
1 tbsp pau-bhaji masala
4 small baps
6 tbsp oil

Ingredients for the garnish:

1/2 red onion – *finely chopped*
1/2 tomato – *finely chopped*
3 sprigs coriander – *finely chopped*

Method for the mushrooms

1 Boil the potatoes, carrots and cauliflower together until tender.

2 Boil the peas separately.

3 Drain the water and mash the 2 tomatoes and the boiled vegetables but not the peas.

4 In a pan heat the oil, add the cumin seeds and stir-fry for 10 secs, then add the onions and fry till they go soft, but not brown.

5 Add the tomato puree, all the spices and mix well.

6 Add the mashed vegetables, the peas and mix well.

7 Add the butter and again mix well.

8 Let it cook gently for 10–15 mins on a low heat and set aside.

To serve

1 Cut the baps into two halves horizontally and toast on a pan lightly covered in oil or butter.

2 Place the vegetable mixture on each slice of the bap and garnish with chopped onions, tomato and coriander.

 # Upma

This is a very nourishing snack eaten for breakfast in Maharastra. It's made with ingredients which are not the ones people would normally choose, but can be surprisingly tasty.

SERVES 4

PREPARATION TIME 20 MINS COOKING TIME 20 MINS

100g semolina

2 tbsp oil

1 tbsp maag daal – *shelled*

1 small potato – *peeled, cubed and deep-fried*

220g carrot – *finely chopped*

100g peas

100g sweet-corn

1 tsp salt

½ tsp ginger – *minced*

½ tsp garlic – *minced*

1 tsp sugar

1 lemon – *juice of*

400ml water

Method

1 Heat the oil at a low heat and shallow-fry Maag daal, till slightly brown.

2 Add Semolina to the pan and roast by stirring for 5 mins.

3 Add the vegetables and the fried potato, then add all the spices and mix well.

4 Add the water and mix well and cover the pan.

5 Cook for 10-15 mins, stirring frequently.

6 Serve hot with salad and a pickle of your choice.

Gujarati Specialities

In this section I have included some of the delicious Gujarati delicacies which are more than just a starter, almost a meal by themselves, like the Patudi and the Khamani. My taste buds could not resist the unique taste and textures of some of the South Indian snacks like the Idli Sambhar and the Uttapam, which I also serve in my restaurant. Hope you'll enjoy my choice as well.

© Rob Booker

Patudi *Plain or Stuffed*

Patudi, also known as Khandwi, is a very light Gujarati delicacy, which could be used as a snack or a starter and could be served hot or cold. This recipe is for a plain Patudi but to add texture and a different taste to it, you could sprinkle some finely chopped onions and coriander before the gram-flour strips are rolled (at stage 5).

SERVES 4
PREPARATION TIME 15 MINS COOKING TIME 60 MINS

4 tbsp yoghurt
110g gram flour
1 tbsp green chillies - *minced*
1 tsp ginger – *minced*
1 tsp salt - *or less if you prefer*
1/2 tsp tumeric to add colour
0.5 l water

Ingredients for Vaghar (tempering):

3 tbsp oil
1 tsp mustard seeds
1 tsp sesame seeds
2 sprigs fresh coriander – *finely chopped for garnishing*

Method

1 Mix the yoghurt and the water in a container and whisk.

2 Take a medium sized bowl and add gram flour, green chillies, ginger, salt, tumeric, and the yoghurt-mix and mix well to a smooth consistency.

3 Take a pan and heat the above mixture on a medium heat setting for 30 mins or until the mixture turns into a thick paste.

4 Remove from the heat and empty the hot mixture on a large clean surface. Quickly spread into a thin even layer, about 2mm thick, using a spatula or any such suitable tool, before the mixture cools down and solidifies then leave it to set.

5 Once the paste has set, cut the paste into strips of 5cm (2ins) by 10cm (4ins).

6 **For stuffed Patudi:** Add a thin layer of very finely chopped red onions and coriander before rolling into rolls.

7 Roll each strip into a tight roll and place it on the serving plate or tray. Do the same with all the strips.

8 For the tempering, heat the oil in a small frying pan and add the mustard seeds. When the mustard seeds start crackling, add the sesame seeds and fry for 10 secs.

9 Pour the oil evenly onto the gram flour rolls and garnish with finely chopped coriander and serve.

This page © Rob Booker

Puwa Bateta

This is a very popular snack which could be a tasty starter made with flattened rice, known as Puwa, which is readily available from most Asian grocery shops. Cooked with potatoes (bateta), it will be popular with adults and children alike. It could be made as spicy as you like by increasing the amount of green chillies.

SERVES 4

PREPARATION TIME 10 MINS COOKING TIME 30 MINS

Small onion – *finely chopped (optional)*
Small potato – *diced*
100g sweet-corn
$\frac{1}{2}$ tsp sugar
$\frac{1}{2}$ tsp salt
$\frac{1}{2}$ tsp tumeric
$\frac{1}{2}$ tsp green chillies – *minced*
Limdi leaves *(curry leaves)*
6 tbsp oil

1 tsp mustard seeds
1 lemon - *juice of*

Ingredients for the batter:

250g gram flour
125ml water
1 tsp salt
Oil for deep-frying

Method

1 Heat the oil on a moderate heat and add the mustard seeds. When the seeds have cracked, add Limdi leaves and the onions and fry till the onions are soft.

2 Add the potatoes, sweet-corn, tumeric, salt, green chillies and mix well, then cover the pan.

3 Cook the mixture, stirring frequently, till the potatoes are tender.

4 Wash the puwa rice under cold running water 3 or 4 times and drain the water.

5 Add the puwa rice and the potato to the pan and mix well.

6 Add sugar and lemon juice and mix well.

The Puwa-Bateta could be served hot or it tastes equally as nice if served cold.

 # Khamani

Another Gujarati delicacy that can be served hot or cold. It makes a very tasty snack or used as a filling for a savoury sandwich with onion and a pickle topping.

SERVES 4

PREPARATION TIME 15 MINS COOKING TIME 45 MINS

100 gms channa daal *(split chickpeas) - soaked overnight*
4 tbsp yoghurt
2 tsp green chillies - *minced*
1½ tsp salt
3 tsp sugar
½ tsp tumeric,
½ lemon - *juice of*
10 sultanas
200ml water

100g fine sev - *for garnish*
½ red onion - *finely chopped for garnish*
1 sprig coriander - *finely chopped for garnish*

Vaghar (tempering):

2 tsp oil
1 tsp mustard seeds
1 tsp sesame seeds
10 limdi leaves - *also known as curry leaves*

Method

1 Drain the soaked channa daal. Repeat the soaking of the channa daal, rub it in the water to remove the starch and drain the water again. Repeat this again a couple of times until the water being drained is clear.

2 Coarsely grind this washed channa daal using a food processor.

3 In a suitable bowl mix the yoghurt, water, green chillies, salt, tumeric, sugar and lemon juice.

4 In a suitable pan mix the ground channa daal and the yoghurt mixture and cook it for 30 mins on a low heat.

5 Let the channa daal mixture cool down for 15 mins and then grate it to give it a coarse texture.

6 For the tempering, heat the oil in a small frying pan and add the mustard seeds. When the mustard seeds start crackling, add the sesame seeds and the Limdi leaves and fry for 10 secs.

7 Add the ground channa daal to the tempered oil and mix well and heat for a few minutes.

8 Garnish with sev, onions and coriander before serving.

 # Mogo

This is my all time favourite made with African cassava, known as Mogo, with sweet-corn, crisps and peanuts to give it a crunchy, chewy texture but savoury taste. A great starter or snack!

SERVES 4
PREPARATION TIME 15 MINS COOKING TIME 40 MINS

450g mogo *(Cassava)* – *cut in small pieces*
225g sweet corn kernels
2 tbsp gram flour
2 tsp tomato puree
2 tsp green chillies – *minced*
100g creamed coconut – *cut into pieces and grated*

6 tbsp oil
1l water
100g peanuts – *fried for garnish*
1 medium onion – *finely chopped for garnish*
100g plain crisps – *crushed for garnish*
lemon juice to taste – *add*

Method for the filling

1 Soak the frozen Mogo in hot water to defrost it and then cut into large chips.

2 Heat the oil in a suitable pan and stir-fry the gram flour, making sure that it does not burn.

3 Add the tomato puree and water to the pan.

4 Add the salt and the green chillies and mix well.

5 Bring to the boil and add the Mogo pieces and sweet-corn and stir well. Cover the pan.

6 Bring to the boil and again and add the creamed coconut, stir well, cover the pan and cook at a low heat, until the Mogo is tender.

7 Remove from the heat and add the lemon juice and serve in a soup bowl with the garnish of crisps, chopped onions and peanuts.

 # Uttapam

This South Indian speciality is one of my favourite snacks when eaten with a coconut chutney and sambhar sauce, but I prefer to eat it with Gujarati Tuweer Daal sauce (see below). The toppings can be changed to suit your own liking, just as you'd do with pizzas.

SERVES 4
PREPARATION TIME 20 MINS COOKING TIME 30 MINS

Ingredients for the pancake:

220g rice flour
110g urad flour
1 tsp green chillies – *minced*
1 tsp ginger – *minced*
1 tsp garlic – *minced*
1$\frac{1}{2}$ tsp salt
2 tbsp yoghurt
400ml water

Ingredients for the Topping:

1 small red onion – *finely chopped*
2 medium tomatoes – *diced*
2 green chillies – *finely chopped*
2-3 sprigs coriander – *finely chopped*
$\frac{1}{2}$ tsp salt

Ingredients for Tuweer Daal:

220g tuweer daal – *soaked for 20mins, boiled till tender, then liquidised*
2 tsp green chillies – *minced*
2 tsp ginger - *minced*
2 tsp sugar
40g tinned tomatoes – *liquidised*
4 dried red chillies
4 cloves
1 tsp Salt
$\frac{1}{2}$ tsp tumeric
$\frac{1}{2}$ tsp hing *(asatoefida powder)*
1 tsp mustard seeds
2 tbsp Oil
2 medium lemons – *juice of*
20 g peanuts *(optional)*
1$\frac{1}{2}$ l water
3 sprigs coriander – *finely chopped (for garnishing)*

Method for the Uttapam

1 Mix all the ingredients to make the pancake batter and leave it to ferment overnight.

2 Mix the ingredients for the topping in a bowl.

3 Heat a non-stick frying pan, brush it with a little oil then ladle in a little of the pancake batter in the middle of the pan and spread it evenly to make a pancake.

4 Cook for 1 min on one side, sprinkle the topping evenly on the top then turn it over and let it cook for 1 min, pressing gently with a spatula.

5 The Uttapam is ready to eat with a sauce of your choice or Tuweer Daal.

© Rob Booker

Method for Tuweer Daal

1 Take the Tuweer Daal, add the tumeric, ginger, green chillies, salt, sugar and bring it to the boil.

2 Take a small pan for tempering the spices, heat the oil and add the mustard seeds, allow the seeds to crack then add the dried chillies, cloves, hing and stir well. *(Beware of a very strong pungent smoke so keep the windows open.)*

3 Add the tempered spices to the daal mixture, stir well and let it simmer on a low heat for 10 mins, then add the lemon juice, stir the daal and garnish with coriander before serving.

Sabudana (Sago) Khichadi

This is a very popular snack in the state of Maharastra. I like it because, unlike the normal khichadi that is made with rice, this is made with sago and potato, which gives it a very unusual taste and texture and it's very healthy at the same time.

SERVES 4

PREPARATION TIME 15 MINS COOKING TIME 30 MINS

220g sago
2 small potatoes – *peeled and cubed*
110g peanuts – *crushed*
1/2 tsp garlic – *minced*
1 tsp ginger – *minced*
2 tsp green chillies – *minced*
1 tsp salt
2 tsp sugar
1 tbsp jeera
3 tbsp oil
1 small lemon – *juice of*
oil for deep frying

Method

1 Soak the sago for 3-4 hrs in water, and then drain the water.

2 Heat the oil in a pan, add the Jeera and stir-fry until its goes brown.

3 Add the potatoes and the sago and mix well, then add the peanuts and mix well.

4 Add all the spices, mix well and cook for 15 mins stirring occasionally, till the potatoes are tender.

5 Serve with plain yoghurt or raita.

Idli Sambhar

A very popular South Indian snack made with steamed rice dumplings, known as Idlis, and a savoury sauce known as Sambhar. The Idlis can also be eaten with your favourite pickles. Idli makers are easily available from many Asian shops or egg poachers can also be used to steam the Idlis.

SERVES 4
PREPARATION TIME 10 MINS COOKING TIME 30 MINS

200g rice flour
200g urad flour
100g yoghurt
1 small lemon – *juice of*
2 tbsp oil
$\frac{1}{2}$ tsp baking powder
$\frac{1}{2}$ tsp salt
$\frac{1}{2}$ l water

Ingredients for Sambhar:

220g tuweer daal – *soaked overnight and boiled till tender, then liquidised*
$\frac{1}{2}$ tsp green chillies – *minced*
$\frac{1}{2}$ tsp ginger
$\frac{1}{2}$ tsp salt
1 tsp mustard seeds
2 tbsp oil
20g peanuts *(optional)*

Method for the Idlis

1 Blend the Rice flour and the Urad flour together then add the yoghurt, salt, lemon juice and the water, mix well and set it aside for fermenting overnight.

2 The following day put a litre of water in a large pan and bring to the boil. Place the dumpling steamer cups on their stand in the hot water. Ensure that the water does not reach into the cups.

3 Put a tbsp of the fermented mixture in each of the cups, cover the pan and bring the water to the boil again. The dumplings will be ready within 5 mins.

4 Remove the dumplings carefully, without breaking them and reload the cups once again and repeat the steaming process until all the dough is used up.

Method for Sambhar

1 Heat the oil in a suitable pan and add the mustard seeds until they have all popped.

2 Add the Tuweer daal, chillies, ginger and salt to the mixture and bring it to the boil.

3 To serve place two Idlis in a bowl and pour a ladleful of Sambhar over it topped with a large spoonful of coconut chutney.

Lilotri - Main Courses

Vegetable curries are very delicious when cooked with the spices which complement their taste and texture. This is the difference between a well cooked curry and a mediocre curry. In my restaurant the vegetable curries, known as Lilotri, are really enjoyed by everyone and most people say that, "if they could cook the vegetables this well then they'd become vegetarian as well." Well now's your chance to practice the art of cooking mouth-watering curries with simple ingredients, by following these nine recipes.

Doongri Bateta

This onion and potato curry is the staple food of most Gujaratis. The sauce can be made as thick as you like it by adding more water or reducing it. It is very versatile because it can be cooked in minutes and can be eaten with chappatis or with rice, especially khichadi (Gujarati sticky rice).

SERVES 4

PREPARATION TIME 20 MINS   COOKING TIME 40 MINS

1 small onion – *peeled and cut into thin slices*

2 medium potatoes – *peeled and cut into wedges*

1 tsp mustard seeds

1 tsp salt

1 tsp red chilli powder

1 tsp cumin and coriander powder

1/2 tsp tumeric

1 tsp ginger – *minced*

1 tsp garlic – *minced*

2 tbsp tomato puree

2 tbsp oil

1/2 l water

1/2 tsp garam masala

Method

1 Heat the oil in a suitable pan, add the mustard seeds and heat until they crack.

2 Add the onion slices and cook till soft but not brown.

3 Add all the spices, mix well, add the tomato puree and mix well again.

4 Add the potatoes and stir well, then add the water, cover the pan and cook for 20 mins until the potatoes are tender, stirring frequently.

5 Reduce the sauce if it is too runny by leaving it on a slow heat for a few more minutes. **Tip:** *Taste the sauce now and add more chilli powder or salt to your own liking.*

6 Garnish with Garam Masala, serve it with Khichadi (Gujarati sticky rice p87) and yoghurt or chappatis, if you prefer.

Methi Bateta

A simple curry which can be conjured up in minutes, when unexpected guests arrive. It makes a great accompaniment with any of the Kathor (pulses) curries, giving body to the broth-like pulse curries.

SERVES 4

PREPARATION TIME 15 MINS COOKING TIME 30 MINS

2 medium potatoes - *peeled and cubed*
1 bunch fresh fenugreek – *finely chopped*
1 tsp garlic – *minced*
1 tsp ginger – *minced*
1½ tsp green chillies – *minced*

½ tsp tumeric
½ tsp salt
½ tsp cumin and coriander powder
1 tsp methi *(fenugreek)* seeds
7 tbsp oil

Method

1 Heat the oil in a suitable pan and fry the methi seeds until they turn brown.

2 Lower the heat and add the fresh fenugreek and stir fry it as it reduces.

3 Add the potatoes and all the remaining spices, mix well, cover the pan and cook for 15 mins or until the potatoes are tender.

4 Serve with puris or as an accompaniment to any of the bean curries.

Tindora (Ghiloda)

This vegetable is also known as Ghiloda and looks like mini cucumbers. When cooked my way, it can provide a very tasty and eye catching dry curry when made with colourful red peppers and sweet-corn kernels.

SERVES 4

PREPARATION TIME 20 MINS MIXING TIME 30 MINS

225g tindora – washed and thinly sliced
1 tbsp sweet-corn kernels
$1/2$ red pepper
$1/2$ tsp mustard seeds
$1/2$ tsp ginger – *minced*
$1/2$ tsp garlic – *minced*
$1/2$ tsp green chillies – *minced*
$1/2$ tsp salt
$1/2$ tsp tumeric
$1/2$ tsp coriander and cumin seeds
3 tbsp oil
3 tbsp water

Method

1 Heat the oil in a pan and add the mustard seeds and fry for 1 min or till they start popping.

2 Add the tindora, sweet-corn, peppers and mix well.

3 Add all the remaining spices, water and mix well.

4 Cover the pan and let it cook for 30 mins at a low heat, stirring occasionally.

5 Serve with rotli, plain rice and tuwer-ni-daal.

Guwar Bateta - nu - shaak

Guwar is better known as the Indian runner-bean and is a seasonal vegetable. It is used to make curries or sometimes mixed with daal sauce (recipe in the accompaniment section) or the Sambhar sauce that is used with Idli or Masala Dhosa to make it more wholesome.

SERVES 4
PREPARATION TIME 20 MINS COOKING TIME 30 MINS

220g guwar beans
1 medium potato – *chipped*
220g frozen peas
½ tsp ginger - *minced*
½ tsp garlic – *minced*
1 tsp green chillies –*minced*
1 tsp salt
½ tsp tumeric
1 tsp ajmo *(ajwain)*
6 tbsp oil

Method

1   Prepare the Guwar beans by cutting off the two end bits, wash them and quickly blanch in hot water.

2   Heat the oil in a suitable pan and first add the ajmo, then guwar beans, peas and potatoes and mix well.

4   Add the rest of the spices, mix well, cover the pan and let it cook for 20-25 mins on a low heat, till the potatoes are tender.

5   Serve with chappatis, plain rice and daal sauce.

Bhaji Paneer

A very popular spinach curry at my restaurant, with cubes of Paneer (Indian cheese). The paneer gives the curry a chewy texture similar to cubes of chicken but the spinach has a smooth spicy taste. We Gujaratis eat it with sticky rice called Khichadi, usually accompanied by Kadhi sauce.

SERVES 4

PREPARATION TIME 25 MINS COOKING TIME 30 MINS

500g frozen spinach
270g paneer – *cubed into 1cm cubes*
1 large onion – *finely chopped*
2 tsp ginger – *minced*
2 tsp garlic – *minced*
1¹/₂ tsp salt
1¹/₂ tsp tumeric

1 tbsp coriander and cumin powder
1 tsp garam masala
2 tbsp tomato puree
1 tsp methi *(mustard)* seeds
1 tbsp oil
oil for deep-frying

Method

1 Heat the oil in a pan and stir-fry the Methi seeds till brown.

2 Add the onions and fry till they are soft.

3 Add all the spices, mix well, add the tomato puree then mix well and let it simmer for 2-3 mins on a very low heat.

4 Add the spinach, mix well, cover the pan and let it cook for 15 mins on a low heat, stirring occasionally.

5 Heat some oil for deep-frying the Paneer cubes and deep-fry them quickly, without letting them go brown.

6 Add the paneer cubes to the spinach and cook for a further 2 mins.

7 Serve with Rotli and Khichadi Kadhi.

Ringan (Aubergine) Bharta

This is another Gujarati delicacy made with mashed aubergine pulp. It tastes divine when cooked well and eaten with chappatis or khichadi (sticky rice) and kadhi (savoury yoghurt sauce). See recipes in the accompaniment section.

SERVES 4
PREPARATION TIME 30 MINS COOKING TIME 30 MINS

2 large Dutch aubergines
1 small onion – *finely chopped*
1 tsp ginger – *minced*
1 tsp garlic – *minced*
1 tsp salt

2 tsp green chillies - *minced*
½ tsp tumeric
1 tsp cumin and coriander powder
2 tsp jeera
2 small tomatoes – *finely chopped*

To puree the aubergine

1 First cover it lightly with oil, then prick it all over with a sharp knife.

2 Put a skewer through the aubergine length ways and roast it by holding it over a naked flame, rotating it gradually so that it cooks all round. Continue this until the aubergine is blistered all over. Do the same with the other aubergine.

3 Slice the aubergines lengthways and the scoop out the pulp from the middle with a spoon .

To make the ringan bharta

4 Heat the oil in a suitable pan, add the jeera and fry until it turns brown.

5 Add the onions and fry them until they become soft then add the tomatoes and the rest of the spices and mix well.

6 Add the aubergine pulp to the spices, mix well and cover the pan. Let it cook for 5 mins on a low heat.

7 Serve the bharta with chappatis or khichadi and kadhi.

Paneer Peppers

This main course is one of the most popular dishes in my restaurant because of the chewy texture, slightly reminiscent of chicken meat-like texture of the Paneer (Indian Cheese). The Paneer is used in North India a lot. It is made with whey milk, almost like cheese or bean curd, which is used a lot in Chinese and Japanese cooking.

SERVES 4

PREPARATION TIME 30 MINS COOKING TIME 30 MINS

300g paneer – *cut into pieces 2x1x1cm and deep fried quickly to maintain its crispness*
Oil for deep-frying the paneer
1 medium green pepper – *thinly sliced*
1 medium red pepper – *thinly sliced*
1 small onion – *peeled and sliced*
4 small cinnamon sticks
8 tbsp oil
1 tsp ginger – *minced*

1 tsp garlic – *minced*
1 tsp salt
$1/2$ tsp tumeric
1 tsp red chilli powder
$1/2$ tsp cumin and coriander powder
2 tbsp tomato puree
2 sprigs fresh coriander – *finely chopped for garnish*
$1/2$ tsp garam masala for garnish
200ml water

Method

1 Heat the oil in a suitable pan and add the cinnamon sticks and let it sizzle until it changes its colour to dark brown.

2 Add the finely chopped onions and fry until brown.

3 Add the salt, ginger, garlic, chilli powder and cumin and coriander powder, mix well and let it simmer for 1 minute, stirring frequently.

4 Add the tomato puree and water and mix well. Let it simmer for 2-3 mins stirring occasionally.

5 Add the deep-fried paneer, the peppers and mix well. Cover the pan and let it cook at a low heat for 10-15 mins stirring frequently, until all the water has been absorbed.

6 Remove from the heat and garnish it with the garam masala and fresh coriander before serving it with baturas, puris or coriander rice.

Ringan (Aubergine) Paletta

This is one of many popular dishes on my restaurant menu. It's amazing what you can do with a simple aubergine, which on its own is quite a bland vegetable. We Gujaratis use it a lot in our cooking be it stuffed, grilled, pureed or chopped into pieces and cooked as a curry.

SERVES 4

PREPARATION TIME 15 MINS   COOKING TIME 30 MINS

2 medium Dutch aubergines – *sliced to 1cm thickness*
2 medium potatoes – *peeled and sliced to 1cm thickness*
1 tsp ginger – *minced*
1 tsp garlic – *minced*
1½ tsp salt

½ tsp tumeric
1½ tsp green chillies – *minced*
2 tsp cumin and coriander powder
2 tbsp gram flour
7 tbsp oil
2 sprigs coriander – *finely chopped for garnishing*
2 medium tomatoes – *sliced thinly for garnishing*

Method

1 Put all the spices into a suitable bowl with 2 tbsp of oil and mix well.

2 Cover the aubergine and the potato slices with this spicy paste.

3 Heat the remaining oil in a non-stick frying pan on a low heat, add the gram flour and fry it for 1 min making sure not to burn it.

4 Place the aubergine and the potato slices flat in the pan, cover it and let it cook until the potatoes are tender, turning occasionally.

5 Serve it on a dinner plate with aubergine and potato slices arranged alternately and garnished with slices of tomato and chopped coriander. It is best eaten with Chappatis or on a bed of plain rice with a side salad.

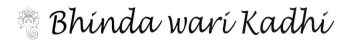 # Bhinda wari Kadhi

This is a really creamy Gujarati curry made with Bhinda (Okra) in a savoury yoghurt sauce and traditionally eaten with Rotlis (Chappatis) or Rotla.

SERVES 4
PREPARATION TIME 25 MINS COOKING TIME 30 MINS

Bhinda curry:

175g bhinda *(okra) – ends removed and chopped into 1 cm pieces*
½ tsp ginger – *minced*
½ tsp garlic - *minced*
1 tsp green chillies – *minced*
1 tsp cumin & coriander powder
1 tsp salt
1 tbsp oil
2 sprigs fresh coriander – *chopped*

Kadhi:

150g yoghurt
1 tbsp sugar
1 tbsp ghee
1 tbsp gram flour
6 limdi leaves *(curry leaves)*
1 tsp jeera
350ml water

Method for Bhinda Curry

1   Heat the oil in a pan then add the Bhinda and all the spices and mix well. Let it cook for 10-15 mins on a low heat, stirring occasionally, then let it cool.

Method for Kadhi

1   In a suitable bowl, mix the yoghurt with the gram flour, the water and all the spices, except for the Ghee and the Jeera, then whisk it to a smooth consistency.

2   Heat the ghee in a pan and stir-fry the Jeera till brown then add the limdi leaves and the yoghurt mixture to the pan.

3   Bring it to the boil on a slow heat, stirring it continuously then let it cool down.

4   Mix the Bhinda curry and the Kadhi in a suitable pan, then bring it to the boil, and let it simmer for 2-3 mins, stirring continuously.

5   Garnish with chopped fresh coriander and serve with chappatis or rotla.

Market stall in Haridwar - Uttar Pradesh taken during one of Hansa's Tours of India.

"The fact that Hansa wants to share once again her culinary secrets for the most delicious vegetarian Gujarati food in Leeds is remarkable. Hansa devotes her whole life to her restaurant and cooking and it shows. Her food is mouth-watering and wonderful and a night in her restaurant is like nourishment for the soul.

Good luck with the book, I hope people will buy it in their millions."

Kay Mellor OBE

Kay Mellor is an English actress, scriptwriter, and director best known for her work on several successful television drama series

"In May 1986 whilst working for a Leeds wine company, I was asked to help set up a bar at a new restaurant. The business was the first of its kind, a vegetarian Gujarati restaurant run by a woman. The BBC turned up to film this new enterprise and like everyone who has ever eaten at Hansa's in the 25 years since, was very impressed.

Hansa herself is not only an outstanding cook, but is also an excellent businesswoman. The restaurant is now a Leeds landmark and it is a huge tribute to her that it has survived (and prospered) for 25 years. I hope you enjoy this second of her very special recipe books."

Best wishes,

Fabian

Fabian Hamilton MP
Labour Member of Parliament for Leeds North East House of Commons London SW1A 0AA

© Rob Booker

Kathor - Pulses

Kathor is the name given to all curries made with beans. I have included here some tried and tested delicious curries which I hope you'll enjoy cooking and eating as well. Please experiment a little to work out the level of spiciness which you like and then you'll enjoy what you've cooked very much.

Channa *Chickpeas*

One of the most common bean curries eaten in most Indian restaurants. Channa comes in a variety of colours and sizes, depending on which part of India they are grown in. They are wholesome, very nutritious and very tasty when cooked well.

SERVES 4

PREPARATION TIME 10 MINS COOKING TIME 60 MINS

450g red chickpeas – *cleaned and soaked overnight.*
(Or 450g tin of chickpeas, washed thoroughly to remove excess salt)
1 tsp mustard seeds
1/2 tsp ginger – *minced*
1/2 tsp garlic – *minced*
1 tsp cumin and coriander powder
4 dry red chillies - *whole*
4 small cinnamon sticks
100g tamarind pods – *see preparation below*

2 tbsp gram flour
1 1/2 tsp salt
1/2 tsp tumeric
1 tsp red chilli powder
5 tbsp oil
840ml water
1 tsp garam masala - *for garnishing*
2 sprigs fresh coriander – *finely chopped for garnishing*

Method for preparing the tamarind sauce

1 Take 100g of Tamarind pods and soak in 280ml of water for 2 hrs.

2 Add 1/2 tsp salt, 1/2 tsp of red chilli powder, 1 tsp sugar and then boil it for 20 mins.

3 When cold, push the mixture through a sieve to remove the fibrous pulp of the tamarind.

4 Use 50ml of this sauce in preparing this chickpea curry.

Method for making the curry

1 Boil the soaked chickpeas on a low heat, till they are tender.

2 In a pan heat the oil, add the mustard seeds and wait till they have popped, then add the cinnamon stick pieces, the whole red chillies and stir-fry for a few seconds. Then add the gram flour and continue to fry, making sure that it does not burn.

3 Add the tomato puree and the chickpeas, add the water, mix well then add all the spices, cover the pan and bring to the boil then add the tamarind and let it boil for 15 mins, stirring frequently.

4 Sprinkle the Garam Masala and the coriander before serving with puris, baturas or coriander rice.

Chevti Daal

This is the most popular bean curry (Kathor) in my restaurant, made with 5 types of pulses. It makes a perfect accompaniment to all the vegetable curries we serve. It is creamy and tasty in its own right, great when eaten with parathas or rotlis.

SERVES 4

PREPARATION TIME 10 MINS   COOKING TIME 45 MINS

200g urad daal

100g tuweer daal

100g channa daal

100g vaal daal

50g maag daal

2 tsp green chillies – *minced*

1 tsp ginger – *minced*

1½ tsp garlic – *minced*

½ tsp tumeric

½ tsp cumin and coriander powder

1½ tsp salt

1 tbsp ghee

1 tbsp butter

1 tsp garam masala

½ l water

1 sprig coriander – *finely chopped for garnishing*

½ tsp garam masala - *for garnishing*

Method

1   Clean all the daals by removing all the stones meticulously.

2   Mix all the daal and soak it overnight.

3   Wash out the starch from the mixture by soaking and draining repeatedly, until the water runs clear.

4   Boil the daal in water for 30 mins till all the daals are tender.

5   Whisk the daal to form a thick broth.

6   Heat the ghee in a pan at low heat, then stir-fry the garlic, making sure not to burn it.

7   Add the daal mixture, all the spices, the butter and mix well, then let it simmer for 10 mins stirring occasionally.

8   Garnish with Garam Masala and chopped coriander before serving.

Magnu nu Vadhu

Vadhu is a very healthy dry curry made with sprouted beans. The sprouting makes the beans softer and increase in size, so the texture is also changed. Often Chickpeas and Vaal (Haricot) beans are also mixed with the Maag beans and made to sprout and then a mixed beans vadhu is made, giving a variety of tastes to the Vadhu.

SERVES 4

PREPARATION TIME 10 MINS   COOKING TIME 30 MINS

220 g Maag beans – *destoned and soaked in water overnight*
5 tbsp oil
½ tsp tumeric
½ tsp salt
½ tsp ginger – *minced*
½ tsp garlic – *minced*
½ tsp green chilli – *minced*
½ tsp cumin and coriander powder
400ml water

Method

1. Take the soaked Maag beans and drain the water out of the pan and place the pan in a warm place to help the Maag to sprout for 2-3 days.

2. In a separate pan add the oil to the sprouted maag (or sprouted mixed beans) beans, then add all the spices and mix well.

3. Add the water, cover the pan and cook on a medium heat, stirring frequently, until all the water is absorbed in the beans and they are tender. The curry is ready when all the water has evaporated.

4. Serve with plain rice, kadhi (see accompaniments) and puris.

   Tip: *Use bean-sprouts (which can be bought from most Chinese supermarkets) if you don't have a lot of time.*

 # *Urad*

A really nourishing pulse curry, very rich in protein and a perfect accompaniment to most vegetable curries. The creamy curry provides the balance to a vegetarian meal, to accompany the vitamins and fibre provided by the vegetables.

SERVES 4
PREPARATION TIME 15 MINS COOKING TIME 90 MINS

220g urad – *cleaned and soaked in water overnight*
2 small onions – *finely chopped*
1 tsp garlic – *minced*
1 tsp ginger – *minced*
1 tsp tumeric
1 tsp cumin and coriander powder
1 tsp red chilli powder
1¹/₂ tbsp tomato puree

1 tsp salt
100g butter
3 tbsp ghee
1¹/₂ l water
1 sprig coriander – *finely chopped for garnishing*
¹/₂ tsp garam masala - *for garnishing*

Method

1 Wash the Urad under running water 3 or 4 times.

2 In a pressure cooker, add the urad and garlic, ginger, chilli powder, salt, tumeric, cumin and coriander powder and half of the butter and mix well.

3 Cook for 30 mins at a medium heat *(or 2-3 hours without a pressure cooker)*.

4 In a separate pan heat the ghee and a fry the onion till slightly brown.

5 Add the tomato puree to the pan and let it simmer for 2 mins.

6 Add the boiled urad daal mixture and the remaining butter in the pan, mix well and let it simmer for 45 mins stirring occasionally.

7 Sprinkle the Garam Masala on the daal and serve with a garnishing of coriander.

Mixed Beans Curry

This is a great bean curry when you cannot decide which is your favourite. It has the sweet taste of the chickpeas and soft succulent texture of the kidney beans, all in a delicious curry sauce.

SERVES 4

PREPARATION TIME 10 MINS COOKING TIME 75 MINS

100g white chickpeas – *boiled till tender*

100g red chickpeas – *boiled till tender*

100g kidney beans – *boiled till tender*

100g blackeyed beans – *boiled till tender*

(Tinned beans can be used if preferred - rinse them well to remove salt)

1 medium onion – *finely chopped*

1 tsp tumeric

1 tsp cumin and coriander powder

1 tsp salt

2 tbsp tomato puree

2 tbsp gram flour

8 tbsp oil

½ l water

1 tsp garam masala – *for garnishing*

2 sprigs coriander – *finely chopped for garnishing*

Method

1 Heat 6 tbsp of oil in a pan and fry the onions till its slightly brown.

2 Add the tomato puree, all the spices and mix well, then add the beans.

3 In a separate small pan, stir-fry the gram flour in 2 tbsp of oil till slightly brown, then add it to the mixed beans, mix well and cook for 15 mins, stirring occasionally.

4 Sprinkle the Garam Masala on the mixed beans and serve with a garnishing of fresh coriander.

Tip: *Add more garam masala if you like your beans spicy.*

"Smile and laugh more"

Bhaat - Rice

Plain Boiled Rice 88

Pilau Rice 90

Vegetable Biriyani 91

Jeera Rice 93

Illaben's Beetroot Rice 94

Khichadi 95

Sandesh's Sweet Rice 97

Sauces to go with rice

Kadhi 98

Daal 99

Gujarati word for rice is Bhaat. Bhaat is very east to cook and it forms a substantial part of any indian meal. It can be made plain or with many ingredients added to it, to give it the taste and texture that you prefer. I have listed many varieties of rice dishes in this section for you to enjoy.

 Plain Boiled Rice

SERVES 4

PREPARATION TIME 10 MINS   COOKING TIME 15 MINS

340g basmati rice
2-3 sprigs coriander - *finely chopped for garnish*
2 tsp of oil - *will help keep the grains separate*
1 tsp salt
2.6l water

Method

1 Wash the rice thoroughly until the water runs clear.

2 Bring the water to the boil, add rice, salt and oil.

3 Let the rice cook on a medium heat until it is no longer brittle. Check from time to time that there is plenty of water.

4 Drain the rice and cover for 2-3 mins. Then transfer into a serving dish by using a flat spoon taking care not to damage the cooked rice.

5 Traditionally a spoonful of butter or ghee is mixed in the rice before serving to give it a beautiful aroma and keep the rice grains separate.

Make time to practice
yoga and prayer. They provide us with

for our busy lives

 # *Pilau Rice*

SERVES 4

PREPARATION TIME 15 MINS   COOKING TIME 20 MINS

340g basmati rice
110g mixed vegetables - *e.g. peas, carrots, sweetcorn etc*
2 tsp cumin seeds
3 cinnamon sticks
$\frac{1}{4}$ tsp turmeric
2-3 sprigs fresh coriander - *finely chopped for garnish*
2 tbsp oil
1 tsp salt
560ml water

Method

1 Wash the rice under the running water until the water runs clear. Drain the rice.

2 Heat the oil in a pan, add cumin seeds and cinnamon sticks. Stir fry until they turn brown. Add the rice, mixed vegetables, salt and turmeric.

3 Add water and stir by using a flat spoon.

4 Bring the water to the boil, and reduce the heat to a low setting. Cover the pan tightly and let it cook for 20 mins, stirring occasionally until the rice is no longer brittle and all the water is absorbed.

5 Take the pan off the heat.

6 Gently stir with a flat spoon. Close the lid again, and let the rice sit for 5 to 10 mins.

7 Transfer into a serving dish and garnish with coriander.

8 Pilau rice is normally eaten with kadhi sauce.

Vegetable Biriyani

SERVES 4

PREPARATION TIME 30 MINS   COOKING TIME 60 MINS (INC PILAU RICE)

340g basmati rice
1 small potato - *peeled, cubed & deep fried*
3 medium mushrooms - *sliced & deep fried*
1 small onion - *sliced*
110g mixed peppers - *sliced or cubed*
110g cashew nuts - *deep fried*
4-5 sprigs fresh coriander - *finely chopped for garnish*
3 tsp desiccated coconut - *for garnish*
Oil for deep-frying

Sauce:

1 small onion
340g tin tomatoes - *liquidised*
1 tsp ginger - *minced*
1 tsp garlic - *minced*
1 tsp garam masala
½ tsp turmeric
1 tsp cumin and coriander powder
1 tsp chilli powder
10 tbsp cooking oil
1 tsp salt

Method

1 Heat the oil in a pan, add the onions, cook until golden brown. Add the tomatoes and all the spices, let it simmer on a low heat for 5 mins stirring frequently.

2 Cook the rice as pilau rice (page 90). Deep-fry the potatoes, mushrooms and cashew nuts separately.

3 Let the rice cool down completely. Transfer into a dish, add potatoes, mushrooms, cashew nuts, pepper, onions and half the fresh coriander, mix well.

4 Add the sauce and mix again.

5 Before serving, warm the biriyani in a microwave or in an oven.

6 Garnish with fresh coriander and coconut.

7 This biriyani can be eaten on its own, with a salad or moistened to taste with kadhi sauce.

Tip: *Leftover biriyani, mixed with kadhi and eaten with hot buttered toast is divine.*

Jeera Rice *(pictured left, top)*

A very popular rice which has a lovely fragrance of the aromatic Jeera seeds as well as the cloves and the refreshing cinnamon.

SERVES 4

PREPARATION TIME 10 MINS   COOKING TIME 30 MINS

225g basmati rice – *wash in water till the water runs clear*
1 tbsp jeera
2 tbsp ghee
6 cloves
4 small cinnamon sticks
70ml water

Method

1   Heat the ghee in a pan and add the jeera, the cloves and the cinnamon and fry till brown.

2   Add the washed rice, salt and water to the oil and bring it to the boil on a low heat.

3   Let it cook for 20–25 mins till all the water is absorbed in the rice, stirring gently with a flat spoon.

   Tip: *To check if the rice is cooked, pinch few grains between your thumb and forefinger. If there are hard bits within, the rice is not cooked as yet.*

Pictured opposite from top: Jeera Rice, Illaben's Beetroot Rice and Khichadi.

 # Illaben's Beetroot Rice (pictured p92, centre)

This rice dish was cooked by Illaben, one of my lady chefs, which I liked very much because it gives an entirely different colour and flavour to the rice. It can be served with yoghurt and salad.

SERVES 4

PREPARATION TIME 15 MINS COOKING TIME 25 MINS

225g rice – washed till the water runs clear
225g peas
1 medium beetroot – *grated*
1 tsp garlic – *minced*
1 tsp green chilli – *minced*
1¹/₂ tsp salt
1 tsp cumin seeds
2 tbsp ghee or oil
¹/₂ l water

Method

1 Heat the ghee or oil in a suitable pan and stir-fry the cumin seeds till brown.

2 Add the washed rice, garlic, chillies, salt and water. Mix well and cook till the rice is tender, stirring occasionally with a flat spoon.

3 Add the grated beetroot and cook for another 5 mins.

4 Add the peas, mix well and cook for 10 mins on a very low heat.

5 Serve with fresh yoghurt and a salad of your choice.

Khichadi *Rice cooked with daal* (pictured p92, bottom)

SERVES 4

PREPARATION TIME 35 MINS (INC SOAKING)   COOKING TIME 25 MINS

170g basmati rice
170g mung daal – *unshelled*
¼ tsp turmeric powder
5 tbsp ghee
1 tsp cumin seeds
3 cloves garlic – *minced*
1½ tsp salt
1.1l water

Method

1 Soak the daal for 30 mins. (Wash and remove the loose shells and drain).

2 Wash and drain the rice.

3 Heat 2 tbsp of ghee in pan, add cumin seeds and let it sizzle until it turns brown. Add the garlic and stir fry.

4 Add the rice, daal, water, salt and turmeric and mix well.

5 Bring the water to the boil, lower the heat to very low, close the lid, let it cook for 20-25 mins, stirring gently with a spoon once, until the rice and the daal are no longer brittle and all the water is absorbed.

6 Add the remaining 3 tbsp of ghee, stir gently and let the khichadi sit for 5-10 mins.

7 Khichadi is often served with plain yoghurt – or kadhi sauce.

Sandesh's Sweet Rice

In South India, rice forms the staple diet for the majority of the people. Everything is eaten with rice as an accompaniment, instead of the chappatis or puris which are eaten in Gujarat and the North of India. This recipe is for sweet rice, which makes a nice change from the usual, to have an offering of sweet rice with savoury or spicy curries.

SERVES 4

PREPARATION TIME 15 MINS COOKING TIME 30 MINS

225g basmati rice – *washed till the water drains clear*
2 tbsp ghee
10 cloves
10 cardamom pods
110g sugar
10 almonds – *blanched and sliced*
10 pistachio seeds – *finely chopped*
½ tsp yellow food colouring
500ml water

Method

1 Add the water, sugar and food colour in a suitable pan, mix well and set aside.

2 Heat the ghee in another pan, add the cloves, the cardamom and stir-fry till they pop.

3 Add the rice and the coloured water to the pan, mix well and cook it on a low heat for 30 mins, stirring occasionally with a flat spoon, till the rice is tender and all the water has been absorbed.

4 Add the almonds and the cardamom, mix well using a flat spoon and remove from the heat.

5 Serve with any vegetable curry or eaten as a dessert.

# Kadhi *Spicy creamy yoghurt sauce*

Delicious with pilau rice and biriyani. A hot cup of kadhi relieves flu symptoms.

SERVES 4

PREPARATION TIME 20 MINS   COOKING TIME 30 MINS

425g plain yoghurt
3 tsp gram flour
1 tsp garlic - *minced*
1 tsp ginger - *minced*
1 tsp green chillies - *minced*
2 tsp amba hardar - *fresh turmeric*
or ¼ tsp turmeric powder
2-3 sprigs finely chopped dill - *optional*

2 tsp cumin seeds
3-4 cloves
10 limdi leaves - *curry leaves*
½ tsp ghee
2-3 sprigs fresh coriander - *finely chopped for garnish*
4 tsp sugar
1 tsp salt
280ml water

Method

1 Put yoghurt in a mixing bowl, add gram flour and water and whisk to get rid of the lumps.

2 Add salt, ginger, garlic, green chillies, sugar and turmeric and mix well.

3 Heat the ghee in a pan, add cumin and cloves. When browned, add limdi leaves, stir and add the yoghurt mixture.

4 Keep stirring until the kadhi comes to the boil. Leave to simmer for 5 mins, add chopped dill and remove from the heat.

5 Garnish with coriander before serving.

Live the

Energy, Enthusiasm

and Empathy

 # *Daal* *A savoury sauce*

Daal sauce is a very popular accompaniment with most meals and rice dishes.

SERVES 4-6
PREPARATION TIME 20 MINS   COOKING TIME 30 MINS

225g tuwer daal - *split pigeon peas*
2 tsp ginger - *minced*
2 tsp green chillies - *minced*
2 tsp sugar
1/2 tsp turmeric powder - *hardar*
1/2 tsp hing *(asafoetida)* powder
4-5 dried red chillies
3-4 cloves

400g tin tomatoes - *liquidised*
1 tsp mustard seeds
Juice of 2 lemons
3 tbsp oil
1 tsp salt
1.5l water
3 sprigs fresh coriander - *finely chopped for garnish*

Method

1   Soak the tuwer daal for 20 mins, wash and boil in water until tender, then liquidise.

2   Add ginger, green chillies, salt, turmeric and sugar to the daal and bring to the boil.

3   In a separate pan, heat the oil and add the mustard seeds and allow it to pop.

4   Add dried red chillies, cloves and hing and stir well.

5   Add the mixture to the daal mix and stir well.

6   Simmer on a low heat for 10-15 mins.

7   Add the lemon juice.

8   Daal sauce is used rather like Europeans use gravy.

9   Garnish with coriander before serving.

Tip: *Keep the kitchen well ventilated to remove the pungent smell when the red chillies and hing are fried in the pan.*

Breads

We Gujarati make many varieties of breads but unlike in the west, we very rarely bake our breads. They tend to be griddled or fried. I have included here a good selection of easy-to-make breads, that will get your taste-buds excited and you'll have fun making them.

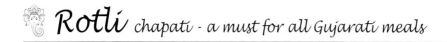

Rotli chapati - a must for all Gujarati meals

Children love them, hot-off-the-pan with ghee/butter spread on them and sugar sprinkled on top.

MAKES 16-17 chapatis

PREPARATION TIME 15 MINS   COOKING TIME 40 MINS

450g chapati flour - *fine white*
Ghee or butter - *for brushing on the finished chapatis - optional*
5 tbsp oil
1 tsp salt
280ml water - *boiling*

Method

1   Combine the flour, salt and oil in a mixing bowl, blend all the oil into the flour using your fingers.

2   Using a little water at a time, continue to mix with a spatula until it forms a rough dough. Knead well with your hands.

3   Use a little oil on your hands and form a smooth dough. The dough should not be too stiff.

4   Divide the dough into 16-17 portions and form into small balls. Flatten a ball of dough into a 2 inch (50mm) patty and dust both sides with flour. Roll it out evenly into a 6 inch (150mm) diameter chapati, using dusting flour from time to time to avoid it sticking to the rolling surface.

5   Put the chapati onto a preheated griddle with a slapping action. As soon as bubbles appear turn it over, and let it cook for $\frac{1}{2}$ minute on the other side. Turn it over again and lightly press the chapati with a cloth, to encourage it to puff up.

6   When the chapati is slightly brown on both sides, remove it from the griddle, lay it on a tea towel and brush it with a little ghee or butter to keep it soft.

7   To keep them soft, store the chapatis in an airtight container wrapped in a tea towel.

Tip: *When baking a rotli on the griddle, only half bake the rotli and finish off on the naked gas flame using some form of a rack to avoid burning it on the fierce gas flames. This also makes the rotli balloon up due to the sudden creation of steam on the inside.*

Khichi Vari Rotli

If you like your chapatis to be soft and supple then this is the one for you. It is a rotli made with a soft rice flour filling known as 'khichi', which gives it that softness. It is perfect accompaniment for any saucy curry.

MAKES 6 Khichi-wari-rotlis

PREPARATION TIME 20 MINS   COOKING TIME 30 MINS

Khichi:	chapati dough:
110g rice flour – *fine*	110g chapati flour
1 tsp salt	½ tsp salt
2 tbsp oil	3 tbsp oil
250ml water	100ml water – *luke warm*

Method for making the khichi

1 Boil the water in a pan, add the salt and the oil and stir well.

2 Add the rice flour to the boiling water and mix it with a wooden spoon till it resembles the consistency of mashed potato.

3 Remove it from the heat and set aside to let it cool. Once cold empty the khichi into a bowl and gently knead it to a smooth consistency then divide into 6 equal portions.

Method for making the chapati dough

4 In a suitable bowl, add the chapati flour, salt and the oil and mix well. Add the water gradually to make the dough, knead it well then divide it into 6 equal portions.

Method for making the Khichi vari Rotli (chapatis)

5 Roll out one chapati dough portion into a 13cm round, then place a portion of khichi in the middle and seal it by bringing up the edges around it and removing any excess dough and smoothing it to form a patty.

6 Apply a dusting of dry flour onto the patty and gently roll it out again into a 17cm round, making sure it does not rupture or leak from the edges. Seal it immediately with some dough if it does.

7 Place it on the griddle and cook it for 1 min on both sides.

8 Brush a little oil on both sides of the chapati and stir-fry for a minute on each side.

9 Repeat the process to make the other 5 rotlis.

10 Serve with Urad or Garam Masala daal and Jeera rice.

Puri *Deep fried bread - a good alternative to chapatis*

MAKES 20 Puris

PREPARATION TIME 15 MINS   FRYING TIME 40 MINS

225g chapati flour - *wheat*

2 tbsp oil

Oil for deep-frying

1 tsp of salt

140ml water

Method

1 Combine the flour and salt into a mixing bowl. Add oil and salt. Using your finger tips rub the flour until well mixed. Add the water and knead the mixture with your hands until it forms a stiff dough. Take a little oil onto your hands, knead well to form a smooth dough.

2 Divide the dough into 20 portions and form into smooth balls. Take one ball and roll into a 3$\frac{1}{2}$ inch (85mm) round, on a lightly greased surface.

3 Heat the oil for deep-frying to a moderately high heat. When the oil is hot, gently slide the puri into the oil, *(see photographs, right)* when the puri comes on to the surface pat it gently with a slotted spoon to encourage it to puff up. Turn it over and fry until golden brown on both sides. Remove from the oil with the slotted spoon onto a paper towel.

4 Repeat until all puris are made.

Tip: *If the puris come out too oily, the temperature of the oil is too low.*

 # Tikhi Puri *A spicy version of the puri*

MAKES 20 Puris

PREPARATION TIME 15 MINS   FRYING TIME 40 MINS

Ingredients as for Puris (above) plus:

$\frac{1}{4}$ tsp turmeric powder

1tsp ajmo - *carom or cumin seeds*

Method

1 Follow the recipe for plain puris but adding the final two ingredients when making the dough.

2 These puris are eaten for breakfast with pickles or plain yoghurt mixed with a little red chilli powder, depending on how spicy you like it.

 # Batura

A perfect alternative to naan bread when eaten hot-off-the-pan.

MAKES 20 Baturas

PREPARATION TIME 20 MINS   FRYING TIME 40 MINS

450g self raising flour
255g plain yoghurt
1 tbsp of cumin seeds - *roasted and slightly crushed*
6-7 sprigs fresh fenugreek - *finely chopped - optional*
2 tsp oil
Oil for deep-frying
1 tsp salt
1 tbsp water

Method

1. Combine the yoghurt, cumin seeds, self-raising flour, oil and fenugreek into a large mixing bowl. With your fingertips blend the ingredients into the flour. Add the water to the flour and form a rough dough, removing all the mixture from the sides of the bowl.

2. Apply a little oil onto your hands and knead well to form a smooth dough. Cover the bowl with a cloth and let it sit for 5-6 hours in a warm place. The dough should rise and ferment.

3. Divide the dough into 20 portions forming smooth balls. Roll them into small rounds (4 inches - 100mm) on a lightly greased surface.

4. Roll a few out and place them onto a cloth.

5. Heat the oil to a moderately high heat in a karai, wok or deep fat fryer. When the oil is hot, gently slide the batura into the oil.

6. When the batura comes up to the surface, gently pat with a slotted spoon, to encourage it to puff up.

7. Turn it over and let it fry for a few seconds. Turn it over again and remove it from the oil and lay it on a paper towel. The bread should be a pale colour but not brown.

Maal Puda

Maal Pudas are delicious sweet pancakes which are made during certain religious celebrations only, such as Lord Krishna's birthday. They are usually eaten with Kheer (rice pudding) and a dry curry, giving it a sweet and spicy taste.

MAKES 4
PREPARATION TIME 15 MINS   FRYING TIME 30 MINS

110g chapati flour
5 tbsp sugar
$1/2$ tsp black pepper – *coarsely ground*
$1/2$ tsp cardamom seeds – *finely ground*
2 tbsp oil
250ml water
1 tsp poppy seeds – *for garnishing*
Oil for deep frying

Method

1 In a bowl add the chapati flour, sugar, black pepper, cardamom and oil and mix well.

2 Add water to the flour and make a batter that is not too runny.

3 Heat the oil in a large deep frying pan to a moderate heat. Drop a few drops of the batter to check for correct temperature. If the droplets come up to the surface quickly, the oil is ready.

4 Take the batter in a small ladle and pour it onto the hot oil to form a nice round puda 8-9cm in diameter.

5 Repeat the process to fry a few at a time, depending on the size of the frying pan, turning them over after a minute on each side till golden brown.

6 Remove the Pudas from the oil using a slotted spoon and squeeze out any excess oil, using another spoon to press with, and then place them on a plate covered with paper towel to soak up any excess oil.

7 Give it a light coating of poppy seeds and serve with Dooth Pak, also known as Kheer.

Juwaar na Rotla (Rotlo - singular)

Most Indian breads are made with wheat flour but rotlas are baked breads made with millet flour, so are particularly suitable for people with wheat allergy. They form the main part of the diet for farm workers who eat rotlas with spicy chaas (lassi), pickles and onions for their lunchtime snack. I prefer it with mixed vadhu.

MAKES 5

PREPARATION TIME 10 MINS   COOKING TIME 30 MINS

225g juwaar *(millet)* flour
1 tbsp oil
1/2 tsp salt
140ml water - *boiling*

Method

1 In a large bowl add the flour, salt and oil and mix it well.

2 Add water gradually and mix the flour to prepare the dough, kneading it to a fairly soft consistency, enough to make thick rotlas.

3 Divide the dough into 5 equal portions and knead them into a ball.

4 Heat a cast iron chapati griddle (or a thick non-stick frying pan) at a slow heat for 5 mins.

5 Take one of the dough balls and slowly flatten it between your palms to make it into a patty, then place it on a flat surface covered with cling film, and slowly roll it out into a 12cm round rotlo. Repeat with the other 4 dough balls.

6 Peel off the rotlo gently, holding it in your palm then place it on the hot griddle with a slapping motion.

7 Let it cook for a short time. Use a flat spatula to lift it off the hot griddle, ensuring that the rotla does not stick to the griddle.

   Tip: *the low heat will prevent hot spots on the griddle, so that the rotla does not stick to it.*

8 Turn over the rotlo to cook on the other side for 1 min, ensuring that it does not burn.

9 Turn it over again and cook again, gently pressing with a cloth, or paper towel, to encourage the rotlo to balloon with the steam inside.

10 Once cooked all over, remove from the griddle and place it between a folded tea-towel to keep it warm. You may apply a coating of ghee or butter to the top surface of the Rotlo to keep it nice and supple. Repeat the process with the other 4 dough-balls.

11 Serve the Rotlas hot because they become hard and brittle on cooling.

Methi na Dhebra

This recipe is for making methi (fresh fenugreek) pancakes called Dhebras. These make a great snack for breakfast or ideal when suffering from loss of appetite when recovering from an illness. The fresh methi has great rejuvenating properties.

MAKES 4-6

PREPARATION TIME 15 MINS   COOKING TIME 30 MINS

2 tbsp corn flour - *fine*

2 tbsp juwaar *(millet)* flour

1 tbsp wheat flour

1 bunch fresh methi – *finely chopped*

1 tsp green chillies – *minced*

1 tsp ginger – *minced*

1 tsp garlic – *minced*

1 tsp ajmo (*ajwain*)

1 tbsp sesame seeds

1 tsp salt

1 tsp sugar

1 tsp tumeric

50ml water

Oil for deep-frying

Method

1 In a suitable bowl mix all the above ingredients, except for the oil and the water.

2 Add the water gradually to the mixture and knead it to form a dough to make the methi dhebra.

3 Divide the dough into 12 equal portions, kneading them to form smooth round balls.

4 Heat the oil for deep-frying at a moderate heat and then slide a few dhebras into the oil. When the dhebras rise to the surface pat them gently with a slotted spoon, to encourage them to balloon up and fry them on both sides till a golden brown.

5 Remove from the frying pan and place on a plate covered with paper towel to soak up the excess oil. Fry the rest of the dhebras.

6 Serve with plain yoghurt and tea.

Puran Puri

Puran puris are another Gujarati delicacy made on special occasions. They are shallow fried breads with a sweet filling, served hot with melted ghee (or butter) or even vanilla ice-cream.

MAKES 4

PREPARATION TIME 20 MINS   COOKING TIME 30 MINS

Filling:

110g tuwer daal – *de-stoned, washed and then soaked overnight*
5 tbsp sugar
220ml water
¹/₂ tsp cardamom seeds – *coarsely ground*
¹/₂ tsp cloves – *coarsely ground*
¹/₂ tsp nutmeg – *grated*

Dough:

110g plain flour
3 tbsp oil
150ml water – *luke warm*
Oil or ghee for shallow frying

Method for the filling

1   Boil the tuwer daal for 30 mins or till the daal is tender.

   Tip: *To check if the daal is cooked, take one grain and pinch it between your thumb and forefinger. If there is any hard bit still left in the middle, the daal is not yet cooked.*

2   Add the sugar, mix well and continue to cook on a low heat, stirring frequently, until the water is all absorbed.

3   Remove from the heat, empty the contents in a bowl, then add the cardamom, the cloves and nutmeg and mix well.

4   Let the mixture cool down then divide it into 6 equal portions and form them into nice round balls.

Method for the dough

1   Add the flour and the oil in a bowl and mix well.

2   Make the dough by gradually adding water and mixing it and kneading it to form soft dough for making rotlis.

3   Divide the dough into 6 equal portions.

4   Roll out one of the dough-ball into a 7.5cm round, place the sweet daal ball into the middle and pull the edges of the dough around the filling to enclose it, sealing it *Continued overleaf >*

by removing any excess dough, then press it gently into a flat patty.

5 Apply a dusting of flour on a flat surface and roll out the patty gently into a 17.5cm round puran puri, making sure not to rupture the skin. Repeat to make the other 5 puran puris.

6 Pre-heat a griddle (or a frying pan) on a moderate heat for 5 minutes then place one of the puris on the griddle and let it slowly cook on one side for 30 seconds.

7 Turn it over and cook for another 30 seconds. Brownish spots will appear on both sides.

8 To shallow-fry the puran puri, brush some ghee or oil on one side of the puri and fry this side for 30 seconds, gently pressing with a flat spatula. Now brush ghee to the other side and turn it over with a spatula and fry it till golden brown.

9 Once cooked, place it on a plate covered with paper towel to absorb the excess oil before serving. We Gujaratis serve puran puris laced with ghee, together with okra curry and kadhi to give a sweet and savoury taste.

Take a 10-30 minutes walk every day.

And while you walk

Paretha *Shallow fried unleavened bread*

MAKES 9 Paretha
PREPARATION TIME 15 MINS   COOKING TIME 45 MINS

Dough as for chapatis (p96)

450g chapati flour - *wheat*
5 tbsp of oil
1 tsp of salt
280ml hot water

Method

1   Make the dough as for chapati dough. Divide the dough into 9 large portions. Roll them into 6 inch (150mm) rounds. Try not to make them too thin.

2   Brush oil onto the rolled chapati and sprinkle some dry flour on top. To create layers in the paretha, lift the top edge and roll it into a tight tube. Form the tube into a spiral wheel shape on a lightly floured surface. Form the spiral wheel into a smooth ball again. Roll out the ball into a 5 inch (150mm) round by applying even pressure, on a lightly floured surface.

3   Pre-heat the griddle to a moderate heat. Place the paretha on the griddle and cook for 30 secs. Turn it over then dribble a teaspoon of oil around the edges and on top of the paretha. Continue frying like this until both sides are golden brown. Pressing the paretha with a spatula during the frying will help it to cook evenly.

Salads and Raitas

Over the years my array of salads have been appreciated by all my customers. Some of them only come to eat the salads from our Sunday Buffet Table. Here's a chance for you to try some of my favourite recipes for this simple but most important part of any dinner table.

 # *Raita*

SERVES 4–6

PREPARATION AND MIXING TIME 20 MINS

½ cucumber - *finely chopped*

1 small onion - *finely chopped*

2 carrots - *grated*

½ red pepper - *finely cubed*

1½ cartons *(22.5 oz/625g)* plain yoghurt

2 tsp cumin - *roasted & lightly crushed*

1 tsp fennel seeds - *lightly crushed*

2½ tsp sugar

2-3 sprigs fresh coriander - *finely chopped for garnish*

½ tsp salt – *to taste*

Method

1 Mix all the ingredients in a bowl.

2 Transfer into a serving bowl and garnish with coriander.

 # *Cucumber Raita*

SERVES 4–6

PREPARATION AND MIXING TIME 20 MINS

1 cucumber - *unpeeled*

½ tsp split mustard seeds

½ tsp green chillies - *minced*

Small pinch of turmeric powder

1 carton *(15 oz/425g)* plain yoghurt

2-3 sprigs of coriander *(finely chopped for garnish)*

1 tsp salt

1½ tsp sugar

Method

1 Grate all the cucumber and squeeze all the water out.

2 Place the cucumber in a bowl, add the rest of the ingredients. Mix well.

3 Transfer into a serving dish and refrigerate.

4 Garnish with coriander before serving.

Sambharo *Stir fried cabbage, carrot and chilli seed*

SERVES 4
PREPARATION TIME 20 MINS   COOKING TIME 10 MINS

675g cabbage - *shredded*
2 medium carrots - *peeled & grated*
15 green chillies - *halved lengthways*
or 1 green pepper - *thinly sliced*
2 tsp mustard seeds
Juice of $^1/_2$ lemon
$^1/_4$ tsp turmeric powder
3 tbsp oil
1$^1/_4$ tsp salt
Lettuce - *to serve*

Method

1 Heat the oil to a high heat in a wok or frying pan. Add mustard seeds, when popped add cabbage, carrots and chillies. Add turmeric and salt and mix well.

2 Cover pan and cook the mixture on a low heat for 8-10 mins stirring frequently.

3 Remove pan from the heat, add the lemon juice and mix well. Serve on a bed of lettuce.

Eat more foods that grow on
and eat fewer foods that are
manufactured in plants

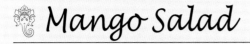 Mango Salad

A tropical salad with a sweet and tangy taste of mango, makes a refreshing change from the usual salad.

SERVES 4

PREPARATION TIME 20 MINS MIXING TIME 3 MINS

1 medium mango – *ripe but hard, cut into small cubes*
½ medium red onion – *finely chopped*
½ red pepper – *finely chopped*
1 sprig spring onion – *finely chopped*
2 sprigs coriander – *finely chopped*
1 medium tomato – *de-seeded and finely chopped*
1 small lime – *zest of*
½ small lemon – *juice of*
½ tsp salt
½ tsp black pepper – *coarsely ground*
2 small green chillies – *minced*

Method

1 Add all the ingredients in a large bowl, mix well and serve.

Sprouted Mung-bean Salad

My very own creation of a refreshing and nourishing mung bean salad that looks and tastes divine.

SERVES 4

PREPARATION TIME 30 MINS MIXING TIME 5 MINS

115g sprouted mung-beans

1 small raw mango – *peeled and grated*

2 green chillies – *minced*

2 tbsp grated coconut

1/2 red onion – finely sliced

1 tsp salt

2 tbsp pomegranate seeds

1/2 lemon - *juice of for dressing*

1 sprig coriander – *finely chopped*

1 tbsp olive oil

Method

1 Soak the mung beans overnight in cold water.

2 Drain the water and keep in a warm place to let them sprout for 2 days. Alternatively you can buy ready sprouted mung beans in most Chinese supermarkets or many health food shops.

3 Remove all the un-sprouted mung beans, de-stone and wash the sprouted mung-beans.

4 Blanch the sprouted mung beans in hot water for 1 min then let it cool.

5 Mix all the ingredients in a large salad bowl and serve with a dressing of lemon juice and a covering of coriander.

# Mixed Bean Salad

A very colourful and wholesome salad that makes a nutritious accompaniment or a meal in-it-self.

SERVES 4

PREPARATION TIME 20 MINS (boiling time for the various beans included) MIXING TIME 5 MINS

100g black eyed beans – *boiled*
100g kidney beans – *boiled*
100g butter beans – *boiled*
100g white chickpeas – *boiled*
100g sweet-corn
1 stick celery – *finely chopped*
2 radishes – *finely sliced*
$^1/_2$ small red onion – *finely chopped*
$^1/_2$ red pepper – *finely chopped*
$^1/_2$ yellow pepper – *finely chopped*
$^1/_2$ tsp salt
1 tbsp french salad dressing - *garnish*

Method

1 Add all the ingredients in a large bowl and mix well and serve seasoned with salt and French salad dressing.

   Tip: *Tins of the all the beans mentioned above can be bought off-the-shelf.*

 Beetroot Salad

This is my own version of a Beetroot salad but with a tempering of Jeera, to give the salad a uniquely aromatic taste.

SERVES 4

PREPARATION TIME 20 MINS MIXING TIME 3 MINS

$^1/_2$ medium red onion – *finely chopped*

$^1/_2$ medium cabbage – *finely chopped*

4 small beetroots – *thinly sliced*

1 tsp jeera

$^1/_2$ tsp salt

$^1/_2$ tsp green chillies – *finely chopped*

$^1/_2$ tsp cumin and coriander powder

$^1/_2$ small lemon – *juice of*

2 tsp Oil

Method

1 Heat the oil in a pan and add the jeera and fry till it goes dark brown.

2 Add the beetroot, cabbage and onions and mix well.

3 Add the rest of the ingredients, stir well then remove from the heat and add the lemon juice dressing before serving.

Forgive   for

The main ingredients for most chutneys -
tamarind, limdi (curry leaves), chillies,
coconut, jaggery and lime.

Chutneys and Pickles

Pickles provide a burst of spicy, sweet or tangy tastes which add the flavour to the food, especially the Kathor dishes, which tend to taste the same throughout the mouthful. We Gujaratis make pickles using most vegetables. The pickles also help to liven up bland sandwiches as you will probably know.

Tomato and Mint Chutney

Simple chutney which can be served with most bhajiyas.

SERVES 4
PREPARATION AND MIXING TIME 10 MINS

5 tbsp tomato ketchup
1 small onion - *finely chopped*
½ tsp chilli powder

1½ tsp commercial mint sauce
140ml water

Method

1 Add all the ingredients in a bowl and mix well so that the ketchup dissolves into the water.

# Coconut Chutney

Ideal with Masala Dhosa.

SERVES 4–6
PREPARATION AND MIXING TIME 20 MINS

½ fresh coconut - *shelled & grated*
or 225g desiccated coconut
¾ bunch fresh coriander - *chopped*
5 green chillies - *more if you prefer it hot*
200g carton plain yoghurt

10 limdi leaves - *optional*
½ tsp sugar
½ tsp salt
280ml water

Method

1 Combine the coconut, green chillies, limdi leaves and coriander in a blender and process until smooth.

2 Add the yoghurt and continue to blend until the consistency is that of a thick cream. You may need to add a little water to acquire this consistency. Transfer into a bowl, add sugar, salt and mix well.

Tamarind and Date Chutney

A sweet and sour chutney, can be used with most starters.

SERVES 6-8
PREPARATION AND MIXING TIME 10 MINS (INC BOILING TIME)

85g tamarind
110g dates *-de-seeded*
1 tsp cumin and coriander powder
2 tsp chilli powder

6-7 sprigs coriander - *finely chopped*
$1/2$ tsp salt
280ml water

Method

1 Boil the tamarind in 280ml water and dates in 420ml water <u>separately</u> for 10 minutes and allow to cool. When cooled mash and squeeze the tamarind until the tamarind is separated from the fibres and forms a thick pulp. Pour into a sieve and again push it through the sieve with your fingers or the bottom of a spoon.

2 Scrape the bottom of the sieve to collect as much pulp as possible and discard the roughage. Repeat the same process with the dates.

3 Mix both the pulps together in a bowl, add salt, chilli powder, cumin, coriander powder, fresh coriander and 280ml water and mix well.

Make   with your past so
it won't spoil the

Coriander and Mint Chutney

A spicy chutney to spice up your sandwich or toastie fillings.

SERVES 6
PREPARATION AND MIXING TIME 15 MINS

1 bunch fresh coriander
½ bunch fresh mint *(or 2 tsp of commercial mint sauce)*
5 green chillies

1 tsp sugar
½ tsp salt
280ml water

Method

1   Combine all the ingredients in a food processor and process. Add water to get the consistency of double cream. Transfer into a bowl and mix well.

 # Red Pepper Chutney

A simple yet tasty chutney which looks great and tastes delicious, providing a nice contrast on the dining table.

SERVES 4
PREPARATION TIME 5 MINS MIXING TIME 5 MINS

1 large red pepper - *diced*
5 tbsp tomato ketchup
1 tbsp salt

2 tbsp sugar
1 tsp chilli powder
140ml water.

Method

1   Liquidise the pepper with the water.

2   Empty the content in a bowl and add the rest of the ingredients and mix well.

3   Serve as required. Any left-over chutney can be frozen till needed.

Bharela Marcha *Stuffed chillies*

This sweet and spicy whole stuffed chilli pickle is unusual because it can be eaten on its own or as an accompaniment to any Daal curry, to give it a kick.

SERVES 6-8

PREPARATION TIME 20 MINS COOKING TIME 20 MINS

Red and green pickling chillies – *slit lengthways and de-seeded*
2 tbsp cumin and coriander powder
1/2 tsp salt
1 tsp fennel seeds – coarsely ground
3 tbsp gram flour
1 tsp sugar
6 tbsp oil

Method

1 In a suitable bowl, mix all the dry ingredients and mix well.

2 Heat 3 tbsp of oil then add the mixture and mix well. After 2 min remove from the heat.

3 Stuff the de-seeded chillis with the mixture.

4 Heat the remaining oil in a frying pan and shallow-fry the stuffed chillis till they go soft.

5 Serve as a side dish or as a pickle. Can be stored in a fridge.

Apple Chutney

One of the most popular chutneys with my customers. It is easy to make and tastes fantastic!

SERVES 4-6

PREPARATION TIME 10 MINS COOKING TIME 30 MINS

1 medium cooking apple – *cut into tiny pieces*
225g sugar
1½ tsp salt

1 tsp red chilli powder
225ml water

Method

1 Boil the apples in the water for 15 mins.

2 Remove from the heat and puree the apple.

3 Add the salt, sugar and the chilli powder and return it to the boil for 15 mins.

4 Let it cool and store in a cool place.

5 Serve with puris, parathas, papads or an accompaniment to your main meal.

 # Carrot Chutney

Can be mixed with fillings for sandwiches and toasties

SERVES 4

PREPARATION AND MIXING TIME 15 MINS

3 medium sized carrots - *peeled and chopped*
2 cloves garlic - *minced*
1 tsp chilli powder
2 tbsp tomato ketchup

Juice of ½ lemon
½ tsp sugar
280ml water
½ tsp salt

Method

1 Process the carrots and garlic in a food processor, adding water to form a thick smooth sauce. Pour into a bowl and add sugar, salt, chilli powder, lemon juice and tomato ketchup and mix well.

Lemon Pickle

Lemon pickle is one of the most common pickles found in Gujarati homes. The lemon pieces are usually much larger in size and the spicy tangy syrup makes a good accompaniment to most curries.

SERVES 4-6

PREPARATION TIME 10 MINS COOKING TIME 40 MINS

2 medium lemons,
225ml water

Syrup:

1 tbsp chilli powder
1 tbsp salt
110g sugar
6 cloves
6 small cinnamon pieces
110ml water

Method

1 Boil the whole lemons in 225ml of water for 20 mins.

2 Drain the water and let the lemons cool down

3 Cut the lemons into 12 pieces (6 slices cut in a half).

4 To make the spicy syrup boil the water and with all the ingredients in it and let it simmer for 15 mins.

5 Remove it from the heat and add all the lemon pieces, mix well and let it cool before storing it in a jar.

6 Best kept in a fridge until required.

Desserts

We Gujaratis are well known for our sweet tooth, so much so that we put sugar in most of our curries, daals and even rice dishes. Having said that, there are some fantastic sweets like the Ghari, Kheer, Shrikhand and Boondi which are most popular because I've reduced the sugar content and changed the way of serving it, to make it more appealing. It really works!!

 # Boondi

Boondi is made as tiny deep-fried gram flour globules, which are dipped in syrup before serving hot or cold or all made up into balls called ladoos. It can be made well in advance and served hot with cream or ice-cream as well.

SERVES 4-6

PREPARATION TIME 15 MINS   COOKING TIME 40 MINS

110 g gram flour – *sifted*
1/2 tsp baking powder
1 tsp ghee
1/2 tsp yellow food colouring
200ml water
10 almonds – *blanched, peeled and finely sliced*
20 sultanas

1 tsp cardamom seeds – *coarsely ground*
Oil for deep frying

Ingredients for the Syrup:

110g sugar
200ml water

Method

1 In a suitable bowl add the gram flour, the baking powder, the ghee and mix well.

2 Add the water and whisk it to make a smooth, fairly thick batter, not too runny.

3 Heat the oil for frying at a moderate heat.

4 Take a large slotted spoon, position over the hot oil and pour in one tbsp of batter. Droplets of the batter will fall into the oil from the holes in the slotted spoon. Fry these till golden yellow then remove them and repeat until all the batter is used up. This is known as Boondi. Let the Boondi cool down.

5 Prepare the syrup by adding the sugar in the water and boiling it for 15 minutes. Remove from the heat and let it go luke warm.

6 Add the boondi to the syrup, then add the sultanas, almonds, cardamom and mix well. These can left as loose globules or can be made up into golf-ball size ladoos.

7 Serve hot or cold with cream or vanilla ice cream.

Tip: *Boondi will last a long time if stored in an air-tight container and kept in a fridge.*

Shrikand *A Gujarati speciality - whipped yoghurt dessert*

A very refreshing summery dessert which combines the succulent flavours and textures of all the delicious tropical fruits. It can be served with vanilla or passion fruit ice-cream.

SERVES 4-6
PREPARATION AND MIXING TIME 30 MINS (EXCLUDING DRAINING TIME)

850g yoghurt - *plain*
175g sugar
1 tsp cardamom seeds - *crushed*
1 tsp pistachio nuts -*crushed*
300g mandarins - *or any other fruit of your choice - drained*

Method

1 Tie the yogurt in a muslin (cheesecloth) cloth and place it in a colander.

2 Place the colander over a large bowl and leave to drain for 9-10 hours. The yogurt will now be reduced to a thick curd.

3 Transfer the curd into a bowl, add sugar, stir lightly and leave to stand for 20 mins.

4 Beat the mixture until it is light and smooth, add the fruit and $1/2$ tsp cardamom to the mixture and mix gently to avoid damaging the fruit.

5 Transfer to a serving dish and garnish with some fruit, the rest of the cardamom and pistachios. Refrigerate before serving.

Tips: *Shrikand can be made in advance and stored in a fridge for up to 2-3 days, without the fruit garnish.*

Shrikand can also be frozen for up to 1 month without the fruit garnish. Defrost by leaving it out for 3-4 hours before serving with the garnish.

Phoebe's Delight

This dessert is based on a very popular Indian coconut fudge known as Barfi. Barfi is usually served as cubes and eaten cold. I find it too dry so I served it heated and covered with cream during the celebration of the birth of my nephew's daughter Phoebe. It was enjoyed by everyone and so found a place in our restaurant dessert menu for others to enjoy it too.

SERVES 12

PREPARATION TIME 20 MINS   COOKING TIME 30 MINS

450g milk powder

4 tbsp ghee

15 tbsp milk

115g desiccated coconut

2 pinches red food colour

150ml water

115g sugar

Double cream for garnish

Chocolate sauce for garnish

Method

1 First make the sugar syrup by mixing the water and the sugar in a pan and bring it to the boil, letting it simmer for 15 min.

2 Take a bowl and mix the milk powder, 2 tbsp of ghee, desiccated coconut and the milk and mix well.

3 In a separate pan heat 2 tbsp of ghee, add the above mixture and roast it for 4-5 min, stirring it continuously to make sure that it does not burn.

4 Add the sugar syrup to the mixture, mix well and take it off the heat, allowing it to cool down.

5 Divide the dough into 2 equal portions.

6 Take one portion and add the red food colour to it and knead it in till the dough turns pink.

7 Take a 20 cm square cake tin, and spread the pink dough evenly into the tin. Take the white dough and spread it evenly on top of the pink dough.

8 Cover the tin with cling film and leave it to set in a fridge for 1 hr.

9 Remove from the fridge and divide it into pieces using a sharp knife.

10 Warm it for 30 sec in a microwave oven then serve it with lashings of double cream and chocolate sauce.

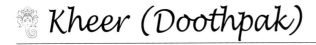# Kheer (Doothpak)

This Gujarati rice pudding tastes divine when served hot or cold with a garnish of cardamom and almonds.

SERVES 4

PREPARATION TIME 10 MINS   COOKING TIME 45 MINS

110g basmati rice
1$\frac{1}{2}$ l milk – *full cream*
4 tbsp sugar
1 tsp cardamom seeds – *ground*
1 tsp almond – *blanched, peeled and thinly sliced*
1 tsp pistachio – *coarsely ground*

Method

1 Wash the rice under running water, till the water runs clear

2 Soak the rice in hot water for 30 mins. and drain the water, then crush the rice slightly with your hands.

3 In a suitable pan bring the milk to the boil.

4 Add the rice to the milk and bring it to the boil.

5 Add the sugar and boil it for another 5 mins., stirring frequently.

6 Add the cardamom, almonds and the pistachio and serve it hot or cold.

Tropical Fruit Salad

A very refreshing summery dessert which combines the succulent flavours and textures of all the delicious tropical fruits. It can be served with vanilla or passion fruit ice-cream which makes it popular with adults and children alike.

SERVES 4

PREPARATION TIME 20 MINS   MIXING TIME 5 MINS

¹/₂ large ripe mango – *diced*
¹/₂ medium papaya – *cubed*
1 Passion fruit – *pulp scooped*
1 Ripe banana – *sliced 1cm wide*

¹/₂ medium pineapple – *de-skinned and cubed*
¹/₂ tsp cardamom seeds – *finely ground – for garnish*
220g vanilla or passion fruit ice-cream

Method

1 Mix all the prepared fruit in a suitable bowl.

2 Serve with a scoop of the vanilla ice-cream and a garnishing of the cardamom powder.

 # Basudi

This is a very rich, thick mouth-watering milk dessert that is very popular in the Gujarati household a combination of exotic cardamom flavourings.

SERVES 4

PREPARATION TIME 10 MINS   COOKING TIME 50 MINS

1¹/₂ l milk – *full cream*
110g sugar
1 tsp cardamom seeds – *coarsely ground*

10 almonds – *blanched, peeled and finely chopped*
4-5 strands saffron – *soaked in 2 tbsp of milk*

Method

1 Boil the milk in a pan for 30 mins, stirring continuously.

2 Add the sugar when the milk has condensed in quantity and continue to boil for a further 15 mins.

3 Add the saffron and mix well.

4 Add the cardamom and almonds and mix well before serving.

Jeera Ananas

A very refreshing tropical pineapple fruit dessert which is so simple to make, and tastes delicious with a scoop of fresh vanilla ice cream.

SERVES 4

PREPARATION TIME 10 MINS   COOKING TIME 1 MIN

1 small pineapple – *peeled, cored and cut into 1cm thick rings*
2 tsp jeera *(cumin) – roasted for 1 min and then crushed*
$^1/_2$ tsp salt
1 tsp sugar
250g vanilla ice cream

Method

1 Mix the jeera, sugar and salt on a round plate.

2 Place one of the pineapple rings in the plate and coat it with the mixture on both sides then place it on the serving plate and let the sugar and salt melt into the pineapple.

3 Repeat the process with the rest of the rings of pineapple, two per person.

4 Serve it with one scoop of the vanilla ice cream in the middle of the pineapple ring.

Tip: *You can use tinned pineapple rings if fresh pineapple is not available.*

Chai-Pani - Drinks

Sweet Lassi 150

Mango Lassi 150

Vaghareli Chaas (Lassi) 151

Falooda 153

Melon Juice 154

Seema's Carrot & Apple Juice 154

Masala wari Chai 156

Aadu wari Chai 156

Fudina wari Chai 156

It is quite customary to offer a glass of water to guests to express your hospitality before any interaction commences.

The two most popular drinks at meal times are water and lassi, a thin yoghurt drink. Water is an excellent form of cleanser and yoghurt helps with the digestion of the food.

Tea or coffee is not usually drunk after a meal although recent studies show that it is quite beneficial.

Sweet Lassi

425g plain yoghurt
3-4 tbsp sugar or honey - *to taste*
1½ tsp fennel seeds - *crushed*
420ml water

Method

1 Mix the yoghurt and water in a large container and whisk to a fine consistency. Add the sugar and half the fennel and stir well.

2 Transfer into a serving jug and refrigerate.

3 Before serving, stir well and garnish with the rest of the fennel seeds.

Mango Lassi

425g plain yoghurt
10 tbsp mango pulp
sugar - *optional*
420ml water

Method

1 Mix the yoghurt and water in a large container and whisk to a fine consistency. Add the mango pulp and stir well.

2 Transfer into a serving jug and refrigerate.

Vagherli Chaas (Lassi) *(pictured p152, right)*

A spicy version of this very refreshing Indian yoghurt drink with a bite, which is quite easy to make and is better than your usual Lassis.

280ml plain yoghurt
280ml water
$^1/_2$ tsp garlic – *minced*
$^1/_2$ tsp green chillies – *minced*
$^1/_2$ tsp cumin seeds
1 tsp salt
1 tsp sugar
1 tsp ghee
6 limdi leaves
2 sprigs coriander – *finely chopped*

Method

1 Mix the yoghurt and water by whisking it for 1 min.

2 Add the garlic, chillies, salt and sugar and mix well.

3 Heat the ghee in a pan and stir-fry the cumin seeds till they go brown and add the limdi leaves and fry for 15 secs.

4 Add this mix to the yoghurt and mix well before serving it with a garnishing of chopped coriander or store it in fridge in an air tight container, until needed. It must be stirred again before serving, because the cumin and garlic will settle at the bottom of the container.

No matter how you feel,

and

Falooda *(pictured opposite, left)*

This is a very popular and soothing milk drink made with fine Chinese rice noodles and Subja (Tukmuriya) seeds, which give the drink a very unusual texture and taste, especially with a scoop of ice cream on top.

4 tsp subja seeds - *also known as Tukmuriya*
6 tbsp rice noodles – *broken into small lengths*
900ml milk
4 tsp sugar
4 tsp rose cordial
4 scoops vanilla ice-cream
chocolate syrup – *for garnish*

Method

1 Soak the Subja seeds for 30 mins in water or till they form an appearance like frog spawn, then drain the water and set it aside.

2 Boil the noodles in water till soft and drain the water.

3 Pour the milk out evenly in 4 tall glasses and divide both the Subja seeds and the rice noodles equally into the glasses, stir well and refrigerate until required.

4 Stir well before serving, with a scoop of vanilla or strawberry ice-cream and lashings of chocolate syrup garnish and a long dessert spoon.

   Tip: *You can also add small marshmallows as a topping to give this Falooda drink a chewy texture.*

Pictured opposite from left: Falooda, Seema's Carrot & Apple Juice and Vagherli Chaas (Lassi).

Melon Juice *(pictured opposite)*

Another simple, thirst quenching drink that's very tasty as well. A perfect change from the usual orange drink.

SERVES 2
PREPARATION TIME 5 MINS MIXING TIME 2 MINS

1/2 medium melon – *de-skinned*
100ml water
1 tsp cumin seeds – *roasted and coarsely ground*

Method

1 Cut the melon into cubes and put it into a liquidiser.

2 Add the water and liquidise the content.

3 Empty the contents in two glasses and put it in a fridge to chill for 10 mins before serving.

Seema's Carrot & Apple Juice *(pictured p152, centre)*

A refreshing pick-you-up drink, which is very easy to make and very nutritious as well.

SERVES 2
PREPARATION TIME 5 MINS MIXING TIME 3 MINS

4 medium carrots
1 golden delicious apple

5cm stem ginger – *peeled*
garnish of your choice

Method

1 Wash the carrots, cut off both the ends and cut in half, lengthways.

2 Wash the apple and cut it into 3 pieces.

3 Put all the ingredients in a liquidiser and make the juice.

4 Serve with a garnish of mint leaf or finely ground black pepper.

Masala-wari Chai *Spicy tea* *(pictured opposite, right)*

140ml milk - *optional*

1½ tsp tea leaves or 2 teabags

½ tsp chai masala - *to taste*

sugar - *to taste*

560ml water

Method

1 Put all the ingredients except for the milk in a saucepan, and bring to the boil. Let it simmer for a minute then add the milk. Bring to the boil again and let it simmer for 3 mins at a low heat.

2 Pour into a cup using a tea strainer.

Chai masala is readily available in many Asian grocery shops but does vary enormously from manufacturer to manufacturer, so please buy only the smallest packet until you find the one that you like the best.

Aadu-wari Chai *Ginger tea*

Fudna-wari Chai *Mint tea* *(pictured opposite, left)*

The recipe above can be used for making ginger tea or mint tea except that the chai masala is replaced by freshly grated ginger (1inch (25mm) root ginger) or fresh mint (6/8 leaves), respectively.

Masala and ginger can also be used together in the tea.

All these teas are very good as 'pick-me-up' drinks, especially when suffering from flu symptoms.

 # Leftovers

We Gujaratis always cook more than is required so we have to find ways of using up the delicious food to make exciting and tasty new dishes, with the minimum of new ingredients.

 ## Rotli Muthiyas

An option for using leftover rotlis (chapatis) is to make mouth-watering muthiyas, but you will need a steamer to steam the muthiyas. This recipe makes 26 muthiyas.

6 rotlis – *broken into tiny pieces*
1/2 medium cabbage – *finely chopped*
110g peas
2 medium carrots – *grated*
110g corn flour
3 tbsp oil
1 tsp garlic – *minced*
3 tsp green chillies – *minced*
2 tsp salt
2 tbsp sugar
4 tbsp water

Ingredients for Vaghar *(tempering):*
2 tbsp oil
1/2 tsp mustard seeds
2 tsp sesame seeds
6 limdi leaves

Method

1 Mix the cabbage, peas, carrots and rotli pieces in a food processor and grind it to a coarse texture.

2 Transfer it to a suitable mixing bowl then add the water, all the spices and mix well. Divide it into 26 equal portions and form them in croquette shape.

3 Heat some water in a steamer to create steam.

4 Oil the plate on which the muthiyas are to be steamed, then place a few portions of the muthiya mixture on it. Repeat the process on another plate, if the steamer has a few separation plates for multiple steaming.

5 Cover the steamer and steam for 30 mins then remove the muthiyas and let them cool down.

6 For tempering, heat the oil in a pan and add the mustard seeds and fry till they pop, then add the sesame seeds and the limdi leaves and give it a quick stir-fry.

7 Pour the vaghar evenly on to the muthiyas before serving garnished with finely chopped coriander.

© Rob Booker

Rice Theplas

Here's how you can reuse the leftover rice to make tasty pancakes, known as Theplas, which can be served with yoghurt or mango chutney and tea.

3 tbsp rice or khichadi
4 tbsp chappati flour
1/2 tsp salt
1/2 tsp red chilli powder
1/2 tsp cumin seeds
1/2 tsp tumeric
2 tsp sesame seeds
2 tsp oil
225ml water

Method

1 Mix all the ingredients in a suitable bowl, except for the water.

2 Gradually add water to form soft dough and knead well, then divide into 6 equal portions and knead it into 6 dough-balls.

3 Heat a griddle or a thick frying pan on a moderate heat.

4 Roll out one of the dough balls into a 13cm round then gently lift it off the rolling surface and place it on the hot griddle and cook the thepla for 10 secs on each side.

5 Brush a little oil on one side and turn it over to fry it, pressing it gently with a spatula. Now brush a little oil on the other side and fry that side as well, till golden brown. Once fried place it on a plate covered with paper towel to soak up any excess oil.

6 Repeat with the rest of the dough-balls and serve with yoghurt or Mango chutney and tea.

Vaghareli Rotli (chapati)

Another quick-fire recipe to turn left-over chapatis into a delicious, spicy snack in minutes. It could be made as spicy as you like by simply adding extra red chillies, to taste.

6 rotlis – *broken into crumbs*
4 medium onions – *finely chopped*
6 tbsp oil
3 tsp cumin seeds
3 tsp sesame seeds
10 limdi leaves
1 1/2 tsp ginger – *minced*
3 tsp garlic – *minced*
1 1/2 tsp red chilli powder
2 tsp salt

Method

1 Heat the oil in a suitable pan, add the cumin, sesame seeds and limdi leaves and fry till slightly brown.

2 Add the Ginger, garlic and the onions and stir-fry until the onions are golden brown then add the chilli powder and salt and mix well.

3 Add the rotli crumbs, mix well and cook for 5 min.

4 Serve with any salad or pasta of your choosing.

Medicinal Properties of food items

I have listed a few fruits and vegetables and their natural medicinal properties as well as the suitability for the three body-types. I hope that it will help you in deciding which vegetables are beneficial to your health and which you must avoid. I have used colour coding in the last column to show the suitability for Vata, Kapha and Pitta body-types in the hope that once you have established your body type, you will be able to see which food items to eat more of and which to avoid.

A – Good for you, A – Enjoy, A – Eat less of, **A – Avoid**

Apples	Protects your heart	Prevents constipation	Blocks diarrhoea	Improves lung capacity	Cushions joints	V P K
Artichokes	Aids digestion	Lowers cholesterol	Protects your heart	Stabilizes blood sugar	Guards against liver disease	V P K
Avocados	Battles diabetes	Lowers cholesterol	Helps stop strokes	Controls blood pressure	Smoothes skin	V P K
Bananas	Protects your heart	Quiets a cough	Strengthens bones	Controls blood pressure	Blocks diarrhoea	V P K
Beans (green)	Prevents constipation	Promotes weight loss	Lowers cholesterol	Combats cancer	Stabilizes blood sugar	V P K
Beet	Controls blood pressure	Combats cancer	Strengthens bones	Protects your heart	Aids weight loss	V P K
Broccoli	Strengthens bones	Saves eyesight	Combats cancer	Protects your heart	Controls blood pressure	V P K
Cabbage	Combats cancer	Prevents constipation	Promotes weight loss	Protects your heart	Helps haemorrhoids	V P K
Carrots	Saves eyesight	Protects your heart	Prevents constipation	Combats cancer	Promotes weight loss	V P K
Cauliflower	Prevents prostate cancer	Combats breast cancer	Strengthens bones	Banishes bruises	Guards against heart disease	V P K
Cherries	Protects your heart	Combats cancer	Ends insomnia	Slows aging process	Shields against Alzheimer's	V P K
Chilli peppers	Aids digestion	Soothes sore throat	Clears sinuses	Combats cancer	Boosts immune system	V P K

Figs *(ripe)*	Promotes weight loss	Helps stops strokes	Lowers cholesterol	Combats cancer	Controls blood pressure	V P K
Garlic *(cooked)*	Lowers cholesterol	Controls blood pressure	Combats cancer	kills bacteria	Fights fungus	V P K
Ginger	Warming	Light refreshing	Aids digestion	Detoxifying	Enhances blood flow	V P K
Grapefruit	Protects against heart attack	Promotes weight loss	Helps stops strokes	Combats prostate cancer	Lowers cholesterol	V P K
Grapes	Saves eyesight	Conquers kidney stones	Combats cancer	Enhances blood flow	Protects your heart	V P K
Honey	Heals wounds	Aids digestion	Guards against ulcers	Increases energy	Fights allergies	V P K
Lemons & Limes	Combats cancer	Protects your heart	Controls blood pressure	Smoothes skin	Stops scurvy	V P K
Mangoes	Combats cancer	Boosts memory	Regulates thyroid	Aids digestion	Shields against Alzheimer's	V P K
Mung beans	Cooling effect	Astringent	Balancing all doshas	Combats heat in summer	Aids digestion	V P K
Mushrooms	Controls blood pressure	Lowers cholesterol	Kills bacteria	Combats cancer	Strengthens bones	V P K
Oats	Lowers cholesterol	Combats cancer	Battles diabetes	Prevents constipation	Smoothes skin	V P K
Olive oil	Protects you heart	Promotes weight loss	Combats cancer	Battles diabetes	Smoothes skin	V P K
Onions *(cooked)*	Reduce risk of heart attack	Combats cancer	Kills bacteria	Lowers cholesterol	Fights fungus	V P K
Oranges	Supports immune systems	High in vitamin C	Protects your heart	Straightens respiration	Combats cancer	V P K
Peaches	Prevents constipation	Combats cancer	Helps stop strokes	Aids digestion	Helps haemorrhoids	V P K
Peanuts	Protects against heart disease	Promotes weight loss	Combats prostate cancer	Lowers cholesterol	Aggravates diverticulitis	V P K
Prunes	Slows aging process	Battles diabetes	Conquers kidney stones	Combats cancer	Prevents onset of strokes	V P K
Spinach	Slightly acidic	Great for cleansing blood	Combat colds and fevers	Avoid if you have joint problems	High in iron	V P K

Glossary

Aadu	Ginger	Fudno	Mint
Ajmo	Carom seeds or Bishop Weed Seeds	Ful Cobi	Cauliflower
Amli	Tamarind		
Athanu	Pickle	Gajjar	Carrots
Atto	Flour	Ghee	Purified butter
		Gor	Jaggery or raw sugar
Badaam	Almonds	Gram	Chick pea or lentil
Bajri	Millet	Gulab jambu	Milk powder balls in syrup
Barfi	Indian Fudge	Guwar	Arrow shaped green vegetable
Batura	Deep fried yoghurty bread		runner bean
Besan	Gram flour		
Bhaji	Spinach	Hardar	Turmeric
Bhajiya	Fritters	Halwa	Fudge like dessert
Bhinda	Okra, ladies fingers	Hing	Asafetida
Chaat	Savoury snack	Idli	Steamed rice dumplings
Chai	Tea		
Channa	Chickpea	Jeera	Cumin
Chevdo	Bombay mix	Juwar	Barley
Chokha	Rice, Chawal		
Chora	Black-eyed beans	Kachori	Thin crusted spicy pie
Chori	Red mung-like bean	Kadhai	Deep frying pan
Cobis	Cabbage	Kaju	Cashew nuts
		Kanda	Onions
Daal	Split bean or pulse	Kara Mari	Black pepper seed
Dahi Vada	Daal dumpling in yoghurt sauce	Karela	Bitter gourd
Dhana	Coriander seeds	Keri	Mango
Dhania	Fresh coriander	Kesar	Saffron
Dhokhra	Steamed savoury rice cake	Kheer	Rice pudding
Dhosa	Pancake	Khichadi	Rice cooked with daal
Dudhi	Bottle gourd	Kofta	Deep fried vegetable or daal balls
Elaychi	Cardamom	Lal Marcha	Red chilli

Lapsi	Bulgar wheat	Ragdo	Thick sauce
Lassun	Garlic	Rai	Mustard seeds
Lassi	Yoghurt drink (butter milk)	Raita	Cucumber and yoghurt relish
Laving	Cloves	Rajma	Red kidney beans
Lila Marcha	Green chillies	Ras Malai	Whey balls in milk
Lili Hardar	Fresh turmeric	Ravaiya	Stuffed vegetables
Limdi	Curry leaves	Ringan	Aubergine
		Rotli	Chappati
Maag	Mung beans		
Maag-ni-daal	Split mung beans	Sambhar	Vegetable daal sauce
		Seero	Semolina dessert
Makai	Corn	Seragwo	Drumstick
Mamra	Puffed rice	Sev	Savoury gram flour noodles
Marcha	Chilli	Sev	Vermicelli
Masala	Mixture of spices or stuffing	Shak	Curry
Masoor	Lentils	Shrikhand	Yoghurt dessert
Mattar	Peas	Soji	Semolina
Mendo	Plain flour	Suwa	Dill
Methi	Fenugreek seeds		
Methi-ni-bhaji	Fresh fenugreek leaves	Taj	Cinnamon
		Tal	Sesame
Muth	Mung like brown beans	Tameta	Tomato
		Tavi	Griddle
Nariyal	Coconut	Thali	Platter (usually stainless steel)
Nimakh	Salt	Turya	Ridged gourd
		Tuwer	Pigeon peas
Paneer	Indian vegetarian cheese	Tuwer daal	Split pigeon peas
Pani	Water	Tuwer-ni-sing	Pigeon peas in pod
Papad	Papadom		
Paretha	Unleavened fried bread		
Patra	Colocassia leaves	Urad	Black mung-like beans
Pilau	Vegetable rice		
Pista	Pistachio nuts	Vada	Deep fried daal dumplings
Puri	Deep fried bread	Valor	Indian runner beans
Puwa	Flattened rice		

# Suppliers

Kishan Stores
20 Carlton Terrace, East Ham, London E7

Mina Stores
274 Green Street, East Ham, London E7

Kwality Foods
166 Goldhawk Road, East Ham, London W12

Sara Fresh
7 Hereford Road, East Ham, London W2

Bharat Food Stores
Carlton Terrace, East Ham, London E7

Toor Stores
160b High Street North, East Ham, London E7

Toor Stores
8 Queens Market, East Ham, London E13

Sira Cash and Carry
128 The Broadway, Southall, London W9

Quality Food Stores
99 Greenford Avenue, Southall, London W9

Quality Stores
6 The Vale, Acton, London W3

VB and Sons
736 Kenton Road, Kingsbury, London NW9

VB and Sons
147 Ealing Road, Alperton, London HA0

Fruity Fresh
133-135 Ealing Road, Wembley, London W12

Shanta Foods
194 Ealing Road, Wembley, London W12

Pick and Save
29 Goldhawk Road, Kenton, London W12

Mandalia Cash & Carry
287 Burnt Oak, Broadway, Edgware, London

Top-Op Foods
Garland Road (EW), Stanmore, London

Jaya Karir
42 Regency Court, Brentwood, Essex

Ashton Sweet Mart (ASM)
Oldham Road, Ashton-u-Lyme

Jalaram Food Stores
46 Showell Green Lane, Sparkhill, Birmingham

Mehta Sunderies
329 Shaftsmoor Lane, Hall Green, Birmingham

Rani Superstores
728 Stratford Road, Sparkhill, Birmingham

Heathfield Supermarket
212 Heathfield Road, Handsworth
Birmingham, B19 1JQ

Yogi Supermarket
Stratford Road, Sparkhill, Birmingham

Masaka General Stores
Stratford Road, Sparkbrook, Birmingham

Surnar & Son
1719 -1721 Coventry Road, Birmingham

Jays Supermarket
21 Pound Street, Birmingham

Michaels Food Stores
117 Hob Mode Road, 95 Ravenhills Road,
and
732-736 Yardleywood Rd, Birmingham

Bharti Spices
Deane Road, Bolton

Raja Penny Profit
220 Deane Road, Bolton

Ahmed Foods
1378 Leeds Road, Bradford 3

Pakeeza Superstores
White Abbey Road, Bradford 3

M.P. Patel and Sons
Arncliffe Terrace, Bradford 7

Lal & Sons
Midland Supermarket, Stoney Stanton Road,
Coventry CV1

Sandhu Supermarket
Foreshill Road, Coventry CV6

Cost Cutters
High Street, Leamington Spa

Londis (Royals) Groceries
Thatch Brooke Road, Leamington Spa

Continental Supermarket
125 Chapeltown Road, Leeds 8

Continental Food Stores
69-71 Brudnell Grove, Leeds 6

Jalpur Millers
137A Harrison Road, Leicester

Madhur's Krooners
307 St. Saviour Road, Leicester

Kisen Mill
23 Melrose Street, Leicester

Shiva Shakti Foods
McDonald Road, Leicester

Nayik Foods
Unit 7, Tithe Street, Leicester

Ghelani Bros
16 Harrison Street, Leicester

Virpur Millers
272 Harrison Road, Leicester

Apna Cash and Carry
Catherine Road, Northampton

Madina Food Stores
Ratford Road, Hyson Green, Nottingham

Mogul Food Stores
Ratford Road, Hyson Green, Nottingham

Tropical Food Stores
Ratford Road, Hyson Green, Nottingham

Anita Traders
Manley Road, Oldham

Suresh Pau-Raghu Stores
Gainsborough Avenue, Oldham

Shah Oriental Groceries
451- 453 Abeydale, Sheffield 7

Shafi Supermarket
68 Spital Hill, Sheffield 2

Patel Brothers
Mill Road, Wellingborough

Index

"I'd like to pay a special tribute to Mrs. Kokila Parmar, who has been with us from day one. Everyone lovingly calls her Masi (mother's sister), who is the head chef and the backbone to my business. She could hardly speak a word of English when she emigrated from Kenya in the late '60s, but had a passion for cooking and we found her a place at Hansa's Restaurant to follow her dream."

Hansa